Eternal Sunshine of the Spotless Mind

Eternal Sunshine of the Spotless Mind is one of the most widely discussed and thought-provoking films of recent years. Bringing together the innovative visual creativity of director Michel Gondry and the trenchant intelligence of screenwriter Charlie Kaufman, the film explores a future where it is possible to have memories erased, and raises many intriguing and important philosophical questions spanning ethics, the emotions, philosophy of mind, and the aesthetics of motion pictures.

This is the first book to explore and address the philosophical aspects of Eternal Sunshine of the Spotless Mind. Beginning with a helpful introduction that places each essay in context, specially commissioned chapters examine the following topics:

- Philosophical issues surrounding love, friendship, affirmation and repetition
- The role of memory (and the emotions) in personal identity and decision-making
- The morality of imagination and ethical importance of memory
- Philosophical questions about self-knowledge and knowing the minds of others
- The aesthetics of the film considered in relation to Gondry's other works and issues in the philosophy of perception

Including a foreword by Michel Gondry and a list of further reading, this volume is essential reading for students interested in philosophy and film studies.

Contributors: Julia Driver, Christopher Grau, Troy Jollimore, C. D. C. Reeve, Valerie Tiberius, George Toles, and Stephen L. White.

Christopher Grau is Assistant Professor of Philosophy at Clemson University. He is the author of several essays that explore ethical issues through film, including 'Eternal Sunshine of the Spotless Mind and the Morality of Memory', which appeared in the Journal of Aesthetics and Art Criticism. He is also the editor of Philosophers Explore The Matrix (2005).

Philosophers on Film

> The true significance of film for philosophy, and of philosophy for film, cannot be established in abstract or general terms. It can only be measured in and through individual philosophers' attempts to account for their experience of specific films. This series promises to provide a productive context for that indispensable enterprise.
> Stephen Mulhall, Fellow and Reader in Philosophy,
> New College, Oxford

In recent years, the use of film in teaching and doing philosophy has moved to center stage. Film is increasingly used to introduce key topics and problems in philosophy, from ethics and aesthetics to epistemology, metaphysics, and philosophy of mind. It is also acknowledged that some films raise important philosophical questions of their own. Yet until now, dependable resources for teachers and students of philosophy using film have remained very limited. The Philosophers on Film series answers this growing need and is the first series of its kind.

Each volume assembles a team of international contributors to explore a single film in depth, making the series ideal for classroom use. Beginning with an introduction by the editor, each specially commissioned chapter discusses a key aspect of the film in question. Additional features include a biography of the director and suggestions for further reading.

The series is ideal for students studying philosophy and film, aesthetics, and ethics, and anyone interested in the philosophical dimensions of cinema.

Available:

Talk to Her, edited by A. W. Eaton
The Thin Red Line, edited by David Davies
Memento, edited by Andrew Kania

Forthcoming:

Blade Runner, edited by Amy Coplan
Fight Club, edited by Thomas E. Wartenberg
Vertigo, edited by Katalin Makkai

Eternal Sunshine of the Spotless Mind

Edited by

Christopher Grau

Routledge
Taylor & Francis Group

LONDON AND NEW YORK

This edition published 2009
by Routledge
2 Park Square, Milton Park, Abingdon, Oxon OX14 4RN

Simultaneously published in the USA and Canada
by Routledge
270 Madison Ave, New York, NY 10016

Routledge is an imprint of the Taylor & Francis Group, an informa business

© Christopher Grau for selection and editorial matter;
individual contributors for their contributions

Typeset in Joanna by
Florence Production Ltd, Stoodleigh, Devon
Printed and bound in Great Britain by
CPI Antony Rowe, Chippenham, Wiltshire

British Library Cataloguing in Publication Data
A catalogue record for this book is available from the British Library

Library of Congress Cataloging in Publication Data
Eternal sunshine of the spotless mind/edited by Christopher Grau.
        p. cm.—(Philosophers on film)
    Includes bibliographical references and index.
    1. Eternal sunshine of the spotless mind (Motion picture).   2. Philosophy
in motion pictures.   3. Memory in motion pictures.   4. Identity
(Psychology) in motion pictures.   I. Grau, Christopher.
    PN1997.E79E84 2009
    791.43'684—dc22   2008054419

ISBN10: 0–415–77465–9 (hbk)
ISBN10: 0–415–77466–7 (pbk)
ISBN10: 0–203–87553–2 (ebk)

ISBN13: 978–0–415–77465–9 (hbk)
ISBN13: 978–0–415–77466–6 (pbk)
ISBN13: 978–0–203–87553–7 (ebk)

Contents

Illustrations

All illustrations in this volume are reproduced from *Eternal Sunshine of the Spotless Mind*, Dir. Michel Gondry (2004).

Contributor biographies

Julia Driver is Professor of Philosophy at Washington University in St Louis. She has written articles in normative ethics, moral psychology, and aesthetics that have appeared in journals such as the *Journal of Philosophy, Philosophy & Phenomenological Research, Philosophical Studies, Social Theory & Practice, Philosophy,* and *Ethics.* She has written two books, *Uneasy Virtue* (Cambridge University Press, 2001) and *Ethics: the Fundamentals* (Blackwell, 2006). She is writing another book, *Consequentialism* (Routledge, forthcoming).

Christopher Grau is Assistant Professor of Philosophy at Clemson University. He is the author of several essays that explore ethical issues through film, including "Eternal Sunshine of the Spotless Mind and the Morality of Memory," which appeared in the *Journal of Aesthetics and Art* Criticism. He is also the editor of *Philosophers Explore* The Matrix (Oxford, 2005).

Troy Jollimore is Associate Professor of Philosophy at California State University, Chico, and is the author of *Friendship and Agent-Relative Morality* (Garland, 2001). His first collection of poems, *Tom Thomson in Purgatory,* won the National Book Critics Circle Award for poetry in 2006.

C. D. C. Reeve is Delta Kappa Epsilon Distinguished Professor of Philosophy at the University of North Carolina at Chapel Hill. His books include *Philosopher-Kings* (1988, reissued 2006), *Socrates in the Apology* (1989),

CONTRIBUTORS ix

Practices of Reason (1995), *Aristotle: Politics* (1998), *Plato: Cratylus* (1998), *The Trials of Socrates* (2002), *Substantial Knowledge* (2003), *Plato: Republic* (2005), *Love's Confusions* (2005), and *Plato on Love* (2006). His paper "A Celémin of Shit: Comedy and Deception in Almodóvar's *Talk to Her*" appeared in the volume on *Talk to Her* in the present series.

Valerie Tiberius is Associate Professor of Philosophy at the University of Minnesota. Her research is in the areas of moral psychology, prudential virtues, and well-being. She is interested in the relationship between empirical psychology and philosophical questions about well-being and the good life. Her new book, *The Reflective Life: Living Wisely With Our Limits* (Oxford, 2008), explores how we ought to think about practical wisdom and living a good life given what we now know about ourselves from empirical psychology.

George Toles is Distinguished Professor of English and Chair of Film Studies at the University of Manitoba. He is the author of *A House Made of Light: Essays on the Art of Film*. George has been the screenwriting collaborator of director Guy Maddin for more than twenty years. Recent credits include *My Winnipeg*, *Brand Upon the Brain!* and *The Saddest Music in the World*. He has also written the original story and co-authored the screenplay of Canada's first stop-motion animated feature film, *Edison and Leo* (2008).

Stephen L. White is Associate Professor of Philosophy at Tufts University. He has published papers in philosophy of mind, epistemology, moral psychology, and aesthetics, and a book on mind, moral psychology, and personal identity titled *The Unity of the Self*. He is currently writing a book involving themes from the phenomenology of perception, which he develops within an analytical philosophical framework.

Note on the director

Michel Gondry was born in Versailles, France. Raised in an artistic family, Gondry began experimenting with animation and motion pictures at the age of twelve. When Gondry attended the art school Ecole Olivier de Serres in Paris, he played drums for the rock group Oui Oui, and directed their music videos. These videos caught the eye of the musician Björk, who invited him to direct the video for her song "Human Behavior." This launched Gondry into directing and he has since worked with artists such as The White Stripes, The Rolling Stones, Beck, Daft Punk, Foo Fighters, Sheryl Crow, Gary Jules, and Paul McCartney. Gondry's innovative videos have used groundbreaking techniques that have become pervasive in the film industry, such as the morphing of images, and the bullet time effect later made famous by The Matrix. Gondry is also an accomplished commercial director, having worked with Levis, Motorola, American Airlines, and Nike. DVD collections of Gondry's exemplary music videos and commercials were released in 2003 and 2009.

In 2001, Gondry made his feature-film directorial debut Human Nature from a screenplay from Charlie Kaufman. After working with Kaufman again on the Academy Award-winning Eternal Sunshine of the Spotless Mind, Gondry went on to write and direct the films The Science of Sleep and Be Kind Rewind, and direct the documentary concert film Block Party. He has recently authored a guide for DIY filmmaking entitled You'll Like This Film Because You're In It: The Be Kind Rewind Protocol and a comic book: We Lost the War but not the Battle; both published by Picturebox. He is currently in production on The Green Hornet, a feature film about the iconic superhero that will star Seth Rogen, to be released in the summer of 2010 by Columbia Pictures.

Note on the screenwriter

Charlie Kaufman was born in 1958 in New York City and grew up on the East Coast of the United States. Kaufman attended Boston University for a short while, though later transferred to New York University (NYU) to study film. He began his writing career working with his friend Paul Proch on pieces for *National Lampoon* magazine, but in the early 1990s moved to Los Angeles to pursue writing for television. While Kaufman found success writing for such programs as *Get a Life*, *Ned and Stacey*, and *The Dana Carvey Show*, his rise to national prominence came with the release of the film *Being John Malkovich* in 1999. That collaboration with the influential music video director Spike Jonze resulted in a uniquely skewed cinematic vision that was also a surprise hit among both critics and audiences. Kaufman went on to win prizes from the British Film Academy and the Los Angeles Film Critics Association for his script, and a flurry of activity followed. Three of Kaufman's screenplays saw release as films in 2002: *Confessions of a Dangerous Mind*, *Adaptation* (also with Spike Jonze), and his first film with Michel Gondry, *Human Nature*. Though *Human Nature* did not achieve the degree of success that Kaufman and Gondry hoped for, they came together again to make *Eternal Sunshine of the Spotless Mind*, released in 2004. Kaufman, Gondry, and Pierre Bismuth shared an Academy Award for Best Original Screenplay for *Eternal Sunshine*, and the film went on to win over thirty other awards in several countries. Kaufman has recently expanded his role to both writer and director with his 2008 film *Synecdoche, New York*. He lives in Pasadena, California with his two children.

Acknowledgments

Many thanks to Michel Gondry for generously providing a remarkably heartfelt and personal foreword that, consonant with the themes of his film and this collection, looks *backward*: both to his memories of making *Eternal Sunshine of the Spotless Mind*, and to his own experiences of romantic loss. Thanks also to Josh Oreck; Lauri Faggioni; Raffi Adlan and Miguel Ian Raya at Partizan; Tony Bruce, Adam Johnson and Stacey Carter at Routledge; and Amanda Crook and Andrew Craddock at Florence Production. Finally, I'd like to thank all of the contributors for their faith in the project, their hard work, and the far-from-painful memories that have resulted from working together on this volume.

Foreword by Michel Gondry

MY MEMORY HURTS

After my father passed, I moved to New York to shoot *Eternal Sunshine*. My girlfriend came with me. She had just finished arranging and decorating my apartment with her insane obsession for colorful and quirky patterns. She had spent a month working on it and we never shared the place. Not a single night. We went to New York and spent a year there. While I was finding various ways to see Joel Barrish's memories of Clementine evaporate, fade, decay, I was building my own with BK.

My production office was stern and quite boring. One day my BK, who was working with us, came to work with two paint pots—a green one and a blue one—and an old book on cats. She asked me to take the afternoon off. When I returned the next day, my office looked so cool. Colorful fabric and cats were sprayed artistically over surfaces of green and blue and the rest of the staff turned green in envy. One of the producers, Steve Golin insisted his office to be subjected to a similar transformation.

Charlie had written the most beautiful screenplay with various poetic ways to feel the memories fading away. I kept racking my brain to find in-camera trickery and visual ideas to match the level of his writing. Also, Charlie had written snow in many scenes that we couldn't afford to create, so we wiped out most of those. Eventually, the coldest winter in 20 years squeezed New York and solidified the Hudson. We actually ended up wiping the snow away for continuity on many occasions.

Meanwhile more fun memories were built with BK. The biting cold engraves the happy moments deeper in the brain than the average weather; it's like a chemical process. Like this time we went to visit Ellen, the Director of Photography, in the snowy upstate, or when we had this dinner in this sushi place and BK overheard this customer commenting on my accoutrement "this guy sure is ready for a storm". She couldn't stop laughing for a while after that. Although not as hard as she did the evening I paraded naked in our flat after a shower making fun of dangling and unnecessary amounts of flesh—only to find myself right in front of our housecleaner, a German activist, in an overly narrow corridor. What on earth was she doing here at 9PM? And why did BK fail to mention her presence? BK experienced a near death laughter moment. She saw the bright light.

Meanwhile, we were shooting Jim on stage rummaging through his apartment to collect all of Clementine's mementos. I don't know why, but I was not convinced by the realism of this scene. For some reason, it felt a bit like a "film moment". Eventually, the crew defeated the cold; we shot the frozen Charles on a nearby frozen lake. It all played out for the best and the movie was slowly taking shape through the chaotic process of editing. Everything was great, until this evening when BK was lying on our bed, so relaxed that she hadn't bothered wearing panties. I remember that was the last time I saw her arbusto. She asked me to stop the shower I had started to run, to talk—decided to put on some panties and stabbed me quietly. She had enough and wanted to be back in LA.

I am ashamed to say that the pain was greater than the one I had felt for my father. Sometimes I was crying so hard in the street I had to stop walking because I couldn't see the pavement anymore. Did I neglect her? I don't know. I think I grew older. I mean physically. BK became more pretty while I grew uglier, or something really pathetic. I was pathetic. I am pathetic. She had left abruptly, saying she had to think and would make her decision in the weeks to come. I knew too well the outcome and the anxiety was eating me from inside, so I went to Office Depot, bought the biggest cardboard box, and packed all BK's clothes and mementos. The next time I watched the film, this scene where Jim is packing up Clementine's stuff was not a "film moment" anymore. Now, I cannot watch *Eternal Sunshine*.

I erased BK's number from my cell phone (to prevent the infamous drunk dial syndrome) and in the past years, I've done the same for the numbers of two other women whose stories ended bitterly. Those three numbers are the only ones I know by heart—because I erased them.

I've read some news in scientific magazines that targeted memories can be wiped out . . . on mice. I wonder if mice experience painful break-ups? So far, technology has only succeeded in making us forget everything . . . except the things we don't want to remember.

MG

Chapter 1

Christopher Grau

INTRODUCTION

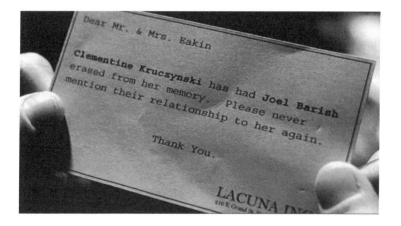

I N KEEPING WITH THE SPIRIT of the Routledge Philosophers
on Film series, this volume brings together both distinguished and
emerging philosophers to explore the many philosophical issues that are
raised in the film *Eternal Sunshine of the Spotless Mind* (hereafter *Eternal Sunshine*).
Arguably one of the best films of the past decade, *Eternal Sunshine* combines
the highly original visual creativity of director Michel Gondry and the

sharp intelligence of screenwriter Charlie Kaufman, both united and inspired by a simple but compelling idea about memory erasure first put forward by Gondry's friend, the French conceptual artist Pierre Bismuth. Utilizing Bismuth's conceit, the film manages to tread familiar territory in a novel way: the classic trope of a couple "divorcing" only to eventually, after some adventure, come together again is given a new twist thanks to a peculiar and powerful memory-removal technology.

The film begins with the viewer residing in the same confused epistemic position as the protagonist Joel (Jim Carrey), and only gradually unfolds to reveal that both Joel and his ex-girlfriend Clementine (Kate Winslet) have chosen to undergo a memory erasure process offered by a dodgy outfit called Lacuna, Inc. The procedure allows those mourning the death of a romance the chance to wipe out all trace of the prior relationship, including all memories of a former lover. Despite having purchased the "spotless mind" offered by Lacuna, both Joel and Clem fail to find much sunshine as a result. What they do find, surprisingly, is a way to nonetheless reunite, and upon eventually learning the true nature of their troubled past together, the film ends with them affirming the idea of giving their relationship another chance.

That brief synopsis does not begin to do justice to the richness, both philosophic and aesthetic, of this remarkable film. Indeed, the diversity of the essays in this collection is testament to the complexity, nuance, and depth of Eternal Sunshine. Beginning with a psychoanalytically informed interpretive essay from David Reeve in which he explores the therapeutic aspects of Joel's journey into his own mind, we move to Troy Jollimore's discussion of Nietzschean themes in the film, in particular the lessons the film offers regarding love, memory, and repetition. We then have Valerie Tiberius's careful examination of the relevance of Joel's memory loss for philosophizing about the nature of the self and the role of emotion in decision-making. Following this is Julia Driver's philosophical analysis of how Eternal Sunshine can help us understand why being erased from another's memory can be seen as a genuine loss to the one forgotten. Coming from a quite distinct set of concerns, Stephen White's essay connects up Eternal Sunshine's themes and style with other works from Michel Gondry and argues that Gondry's cinematic innovations do much more than entertain: they challenge a number of misguided philosophical approaches to film and to perception, and they suggest the virtues of a neglected phenomenological alternative. Finally,

George Toles offers a moving and personal essay that considers the ways in which *Eternal Sunshine* can remind us of the capacity of memory and imagination to truly engage with those closest to us.

In Noël Carroll's introduction to the Philosophers on Film volume on *Talk to Her*, he helpfully distinguishes between a number of different ways in which philosophers can interact with film: while some philosophers tackle the specific philosophical questions that arise when considering film as an art form, others utilize the content of particular films as jumping off points in order to explore more general philosophical ideas, ideas that may be merely suggested (perhaps unintentionally) on the screen.[1] Others still make the case that the films themselves can philosophize: the claim here is that, while obviously not in the business of providing proofs or giving explicit theoretical arguments, some films nonetheless not only raise philosophical questions but suggest answers to those questions. Though philosophers sometimes talk loosely about such categories as though they are exclusive in nature, Carroll is clearly right to avoid this, and attempting to apply these categories to the contributions in this collection helps highlight why. Consider White's essay: it explores some classic issues in film theory, and so in that respect it falls pretty neatly into the first category (what Carroll calls "philosophy of motion pictures"), but White also provides grounds for thinking of Gondry's work as engaged in philosophy in its own right, and thus his essay fits Carroll's third category (what some have called "film *as* philosophy"). Reeve's, Jollimore's, and Toles's essays seem to me to criss-cross the boundaries of "film as philosophy," "philosophy of motion pictures," and Carroll's second category (which he calls "philosophy *in* film"), all the while offering and defending interpretive claims that would be at home in the longstanding tradition of theoretically informed film criticism written by non-philosophers. Both Driver's and Tiberius's essays fit fairly well into the "philosophy in film" camp, but that label could be misleading by suggesting that they aren't offering up original philosophical work in addition to demonstrating connections between the film and standard philosophical issues.

In the end what matters most to me about all of the essays here is not which of these categories they best fit, but that they each help to show, often in quite different ways, why *Eternal Sunshine* is a film that is not just worth seeing but worth dwelling on, puzzling over, and living with through repeated examination. Of course, one need not be a philosopher to reflect usefully on a film such as *Eternal Sunshine*, but what the essays in this collection all have in common is a serious and sustained passion for rigor, truth, and the uncovering of value that is the hallmark of good philosophical writing since the time of Plato. I hope you'll agree that when this philosophical spirit is directed at a film as rewarding of reflection as *Eternal Sunshine*, the results can be impressive.

David Reeve begins his essay "Two Blue Ruins: Love and Memory in *Eternal Sunshine of the Spotless Mind*" by acknowledging that *Eternal Sunshine* naturally prompts viewers to dwell on philosophical questions raised by memory erasure, but he suggests that the film itself is not primarily engaged in that particular investigation. Rather, he argues forcefully that the direction of the film's own thought is towards love and its roots in childhood. Adopting a broadly Freudian focus, Reeve provides an interpretation that highlights the ways in which *Eternal Sunshine* repeatedly and carefully lingers over such topics as the role our childhood plays in forming our capacity to love, as well as how that same childhood shapes our conception of who it is we are most inclined to love. Not surprisingly, he is particularly interested in those sequences of the film in which we return to Joel's youth and are shown his formative childhood anxieties and desires. Reeve also explores how these same psychoanalytic themes crop up throughout the film and are embodied in connections as subtle as the one between Joel's admission to a fondness for his childhood Huckleberry Hound doll and his (not altogether ineffective) tendency to adopt a "wounded puppy" pose when dealing with Clementine.

Surely part of the appeal of *Eternal Sunshine* for many viewers is that it provides its own spin on the traditional Hollywood tactic of playing on the deep-seated wish lovers often have for second chances. Many a classic romantic comedy has followed the formula of offering us visions of couples who end up getting that inspiring (if improbable) chance to "do it all again," and we root for them to succeed in the replay that is so rarely available to us in real life. *Eternal Sunshine* is complex and ambiguous enough that there are a variety of ways in which a viewer can interpret the possibilities for renewed and improved love offered to the couple. Those of a pessimistic bent are likely to see Joel and Clementine as simply doomed to repeat the same mistakes yet again (and perhaps again and again and again . . .). Most, however, see the film as offering a more hopeful vision, but even here there's room for disagreement over why hope is in place.

Perhaps the most straightforward interpretation is centered on the notion that optimism is justified because the couple's memories of each other went deeper than Lacuna could ever reach, and thus, post-erasure, they are still in a position to genuinely benefit from their shared past and some knowledge of their previous mistakes. Reeve offers support for such an analysis in pointing to both the implausibly radical scope of Lacuna's goals and the slipshod nature of their actual operation. However, the heart of his essay explores the more interesting possibility that hope is warranted primarily because of a beneficial therapeutic transformation achieved in the course of Joel (self-consciously) undergoing the memory erasure procedure. In other words, the unusual opportunity offered to him to relive and rework the past puts him in a better position to recognize both Clementine's actual worth and the reasons why his own psychic limitations had previously led him to distort her nature and her importance to him.

Reeve's thesis, which brings with it the claim that Joel alone was in need of such therapy, while Clementine "already has the sort of heart that Joel, through suffering, must acquire," is bound to strike some as controversial. It is backed up with considerable skill, however, and takes for ammunition the credible insight that when they first came together Joel too quickly adopted a picture of Clementine as a savior who would do all the necessary heavy lifting to inject much-needed sunshine into his life. Joel's conscious absorption into Lacuna's process of erasure, and the trip to his past it allows, gets him to see that Clementine's real aid comes in the form of a partner who can help *mend* him rather than simply *soothe* him. As they go through assorted memories of both their relationship and his childhood we see her, as teacher and guide, direct him to adopt a healthier and more mature perspective on his life, his limitations, and his love for her. Reeve's careful consideration of the film reveals that at the core of this narrative resides an unexpectedly curative journey of self-discovery for Joel. This is a journey that, through the talents of Gondry and Kaufman, manages to take on a thrilling and powerfully cinematic dimension for the viewer, a dimension rarely achieved in such a complex and philosophical tale of psychic renovation.

We saw that David Reeve's interpretation of *Eternal Sunshine* presupposed the potential for *hope* at the end of the film: the couple's affirmation and willingness to continue their relationship seems to derive in part from the expectation that things just might go better this time. Reeve's reasons for optimism are not exhausted by an awareness of the possibility of Joel and Clem drawing on residual memories, or the access the couple has to the knowledge contained in returned tapes. Rather, Reeve suggests that the particularities of Joel's erasure process have allowed him to come out of that procedure psychically transformed, and thus in a better position to pursue a relationship with Clementine than when they first met.

While I think many viewers do take the film to contain a "happy ending," and I think they respond this way in part because they leave the theater thinking that *perhaps* Joel and Clementine will avoid some of the mistakes (and resulting heartache) that plagued them the first time around, I'm also impressed by Troy Jollimore's audacious suggestion that there is a sense in which the film ought to be seen as ending happily *even if the couple is in fact doomed to repeat every last mistake and sorrow*. In "Miserably Ever After: Forgetting, Repeating, and Affirming Love in *Eternal Sunshine of the Spotless Mind*," Jollimore presents an extended discussion of Nietzschean themes in *Eternal Sunshine*. In particular (and as the title suggests) he focuses on the importance for Nietzsche of the idea of *affirming* one's life even in the face of great difficulty.

Jollimore proposes four "affirmation theses," derived from Nietzsche's writings, that have relevance for our understanding of *Eternal Sunshine*. Briefly, these theses can be summarized as follows: 1) Affirming one's life necessarily involves denying and forgetting certain aspects of that life and of reality more generally. 2) When one can, one *ought to* affirm even the painful aspects of one's life, for denying reality is a sign of weakness. 3) To affirm certain moments in one's life is inevitably to affirm the *whole* life. 4) One ought to affirm life *as it is lived*, in the present, and resist the temptation to evaluate the moment with reference to some general standard derived from either the past or the future.

In a wide-ranging discussion that draws on such diverse literary sources as Lydia Davis, Milan Kundera, R. W. Emerson, and C. S. Lewis, Jollimore considers the ways in which these four theses capture provocative but nonetheless genuine insights about the importance of affirmation in life and in love. Pointing out that it is far from clear that the theses can be brought together into a systematic whole, he explains that such systematization was not Nietzsche's goal. Indeed, as Jollimore describes it, the fourth thesis contains within it a recommendation from Nietzsche that we *resist* the natural and strong urge to impose such a framework on either our lives or our philosophical thought. Jollimore takes this fourth thesis to resonate with aspects of Emerson's thought, and he declares it to be both the most important and the most troubling thesis of the lot. He then considers the multiple ways in which *Eternal Sunshine* shows Clementine (and sometimes Joel) embodying this call to resist consistency and accept the present moment.

Jollimore ends his essay with an examination of Nietzsche's famous doctrine of the eternal return, and draws connections between the model of affirmation presented in that parable and the endorsement and affirmation we see in the "okays" exchanged by Joel and Clementine in the final moments of the film. The couple's readiness to say "okay" (in light of the knowledge that any attempt at a new relationship is surely doomed) is offered by Jollimore as testament to their courage, their wisdom, and their love. As viewers, he asks us to reconsider our willingness to recoil at the thought of the two throwing themselves into a painful repetition of past mistakes. Instead, he argues that we take seriously the idea that such a miserable outcome for the couple is wholly compatible with their final affirmation, and that this affirmation, made while aware of the dark future that lay before them, provides a joyous finale to what Jollimore considers "one of the most romantic movies ever made."

Valerie Tiberius is a philosopher whose work has focused on theories of practical reasoning and philosophical conceptions of the role of reflection in a good life. Her contribution to this collection, "Bad Memories, Good Decisions, and the Three Joels," utilizes *Eternal Sunshine* as a vehicle for exploring some of the theoretical questions that arise when we try to determine how best to make decisions about our lives. Pointing out the ways in which the film vividly presents important psychological truths about the dangers of memory distortion and the role of emotion in decision-making, Tiberius helpfully sketches an account of "three Joels" that we are presented with in *Eternal Sunshine*: a "bitter" Joel, who is under the influence of powerful angry emotions after a difficult break-up; a "spotless" Joel, who has had memories of his relationship erased; and the "sadder but wiser" Joel, who has had his memories erased but learned about this (and other aspects of his relationship with Clem) through listening to the returned tapes. By considering which of these Joels is best placed to make decisions about a future relationship with Clementine, Tiberius leads the reader to explore various philosophical approaches to decision-making, approaches that, at least initially, may appear to be in tension with each other.

Tiberius points out that it is pretty clear that "spotless Joel," with his memories of the previous relationship wiped clean, is missing information crucial to making the best decision about a future with Clementine. Does it follow that "bitter Joel" is in the best position to judge the merits of the situation? Probably not, as bitter Joel appears to be experiencing the sort of memory distortion and emotional overload that psychologists have shown to be typical: we naturally focus on the peak and end of our memories, and Joel's anger and fixation on the bitter end of his relationship with Clementine does not seem to put him in the best position to consider whether a future with her is possible or desirable.

This leaves us with the inference that "sadder but wiser" Joel is in fact best placed to decide on a future relationship with Clementine. Tiberius does indeed endorse this apparently common-sense conclusion, but she cautions that whether the "calm, cool" perspective afforded this Joel is ideal depends in part on the particular circumstances in which he has found himself. Given the nature of their relationship and the path that brought Joel and Clem together again, Joel is better off having some distance from his anger, as this buffer allows him to correctly see the potential for a more successful relationship the second time around. However, Tiberius points out that had things been different—consider, for example, the possibility that their initial relationship was seriously abusive—perhaps bitter Joel (or bitter Clem) would have been in the best position to make a wise decision. Anger triggered by memories of such a past would arguably not be distorting one's vision but rather clarifying it. Tiberius argues persuasively that while it is good to have distance from distorting memories and emotions, not all memories are distorted, and the emotions triggered by memories need not always be discounted as suspect. Given her embrace of a contextual approach to decision-making that acknowledges the virtues of both a distanced perspective and the insight that can be provided by emotion, Tiberius concludes her discussion with a consideration of the worry that the flexibility required of her account is at odds with our ordinary sense of ourselves as unified authors of our lives. Criticizing the robust notion of unity demanded by philosophers such as Christine Korsgaard, Tiberius makes the case that a nuanced vision of the self as involving multiple perspectives is better able to make sense of our own experiences as agents and, in addition, she suggests that this approach offers a framework for making more humane judgments regarding the decisions and behavior of others. Tiberius credits *Eternal Sunshine* with helping us to philosophize about these important issues through presenting us with a creative and powerful depiction of the various perspectives available to Joel Barish in the course of the film.

Like Tiberius, Julia Driver is interested in reflecting on the philosophical relevance of the memory erasure technology depicted in *Eternal Sunshine*. However, rather than focus on how memory loss might affect one's ability to make good decisions, Driver's essay, "Memory, Desire, and Value in *Eternal Sunshine of the Spotless Mind*," considers the nature and scope of the possible harms involved in such a loss. More specifically, she explores the philosophical issues connected to the belief that Clementine's erasure of memories of Joel constitutes a harm *to Joel*. How is it that someone else's decision to erase a memory of you could amount to a harm to you? Driver begins her essay with a discussion of some of the relevant arguments offered by the philosopher Avishai Margalit, whose book *The Ethics of Memory* is one of the few sustained philosophical treatments of these sorts of questions. Margalit makes the case that the moral importance of memory is essentially linked to its importance in creating and maintaining "thick" relationships with others. (Such relations are typically those substantial and personal relations we have to those close to us.) While sympathetic to Margalit's emphasis on the connection between memory and the care that cements thick relations, Driver goes on to offer her own independent and original arguments for why memory loss can be a harm and how, in particular, such a loss can be a harm to the one forgotten.

Driver's discussion centers around a thought experiment in which we are asked to consider the nature of the loss incurred to a skier who suffers an accident that results in total loss of his memories of his wife and children. Imagining that the man can, upon recovering from the accident, be informed of all the relevant details of his relationships to his family, we realize that something very significant has nonetheless been sacrificed. While he'll come to have "propositional knowledge" of his past with these people, he won't be able to regain the actual memories, and thus he won't regain the specific emotional connections to his loved ones that those memories made possible. Pointing out the parallels between such a scenario and the situation Joel and Clementine find themselves in at the end of *Eternal Sunshine*, Driver considers the ramifications of such a loss both for the amnesic and those forgotten.

In focusing on the ways in which memory loss cuts a person off from the specific attachments they have to others, Driver makes the case that those cut off can rightly complain of being harmed when the forgotten individuals possess a desire to be remembered. However, not just any such desire will do: drawing on the work of Derek Parfit, Driver explains how some such desires to be remembered may not actually be "operational" in the life of the individual possessing the desire. In other words, one might have desires that float free of one's other concerns, projects, and values. In such a case, the failure for the desire to be realized may not matter much, and may not amount to a significant harm. In the case of a desire to be remembered by a loved one (or ex-loved one, as in the case of Joel's desire to be remembered by Clementine) it seems clear that what is at stake is a desire that is operational, one that meshes with important parts of one's life, and thus Driver concludes that we can philosophically defend the intuitive idea that Clementine's memory erasure amounts to a genuine loss for Joel.

Stephen White's essay, "Michel Gondry and the Phenomenology of Visual Perception," takes a different tack from the other essays in this collection by considering *Eternal Sunshine* in the context of other works by Michel Gondry. The essay begins by pointing out some underappreciated similarities between one important "realist" strain of film theory (according to which the cinematic image is a particularly objective record of reality) and the still-influential approach in philosophy of mind that understands perception as involving the unmediated reception of raw sensory data. White then goes on to offer a thorough demonstration of the many ways in which the work of Michel Gondry challenges both philosophical dogmas. Considering *Eternal Sunshine* alongside Gondry's many music videos and his more recent film *The Science of Sleep*, White catalogues the variety of techniques through which Gondry repeatedly upsets comfortable philosophical assumptions by utilizing highly creative manipulations of the images that appear within a movie frame.

In his music videos, Gondry forces viewers to become aware of their implicit assumptions about both cinematic and ordinary perception by offering surprising reversals: optical effects manifest literal "traces" in space and time; doublings and repetitions that could be easily accomplished through optical or digital effects are achieved manually; typical patterns of causation are turned around; and spatial norms are persistently violated. Eternal Sunshine, seen in the light of these other experiments, functions as a "kind of negative image of his short films." The many sequences in the film that visualize memory erasure through a gradual dismantling of the field of perception (e.g. the slow fading away of the books in the bookstore) remind us of just how full of significance the ordinary film image is. This, in turn, can remind us that ordinary perception itself is not in fact a passive process in which we are given raw "sense-data." Instead, it is always already experienced under a variety of fundamental categories and distinctions, such as the categories of time and intentionality and the distinctions between inside/outside and self/other. Eternal Sunshine, in particular, offers an invitation to consider the multiple ways in which "the past is given to us in its traces in the present." White convincingly argues that Gondry's "philosophical film practice" can help us to appreciate an important phenomenological insight: we naturally and directly perceive zones of significance and traces of the past in a way that is not adequately appreciated by either realist film theory or the empiricist tradition in the philosophy of perception. On this account, watching Eternal Sunshine can be, among many other things, a helpful dose of philosophical therapy.

There is a moment on the commentary track when Charlie Kaufman remarks that, in the scene being shown, Clementine is actually (and merely) a projection of Joel's mind. As he puts it: "Clementine is really Joel talking to himself." Kaufman goes on to suggest that this quirk of the plot allows Joel license to be more adventurous than he might otherwise. Michel Gondry, while not exactly disagreeing with Kaufman's remarks, suggests instead that "sometimes when you talk to people in your head you can find a way to talk for real to them." He then goes on to give a touching elaboration of this thought:

> I had this experience when my father was dying [. . .] I remember talking to him in my head at this time when you wake up in the morning [. . .] and I could really have a conversation with him . . . and I thought that maybe all the information I had from him were

collected at this moment by my subconscious and I would put them all together and I reconstruct his character in a way that I was not necessarily aware of . . . so I think there is a possibility to talk to somebody even if it is in your imagination [. . .] it is kind of tricky . . . it is like people would think when you experience afterlife stuff, but I just think that's rubbish.[2]

There is a bold suggestion here that our imaginative engagement (in dreams, memories, or daydreams) with those close to us allows for access to real truths about those persons, truths perhaps otherwise unavailable. This provocative idea lies at the core of George Toles's contribution to this volume, "Trying to Remember Clementine." Toles begins his essay with a consideration of some remarks from Kaufman that represent the more skeptical (and quite common) view that memories, far from providing mirrors of the past, offer up instead an inevitably skewed and thus suspect projection. Toles later connects this seemingly sophisticated cynicism about memory with the related Proustian worry that a focus honed through love and attachment distorts rather than clarifies the object of our vision. He challenges these ideas and, in what I take to be a thoroughly Gondry-esque spirit, offers up an extensive discussion of *Eternal Sunshine* in which we are asked to seriously consider the possibility that Joel's engagement with his memories of Clementine make possible a level of careful, loving attention and knowledge that is often *not* possible when we encounter a person "face to face."

Devoting much of his attention to the scene in which Joel and Clementine return home from Montauk on the train, Toles explores the nuanced ways in which the characters struggle in those moments to stagger forward (unaware of their recent mental impoverishment) while inevitably, if unconsciously, being moved by their nature and what remains of their memories to connect again. Seeing both of them as unknowingly enduring a process of mourning, Toles considers how in "a landscape chilled by bereavement" Joel and Clementine are able to slowly and hesitantly come to reveal themselves to each other and, in turn, to themselves.

Of course, the first time through the film we are as ignorant as the characters of their loss and bereavement. It is only on later viewings that the impressive subtlety and importance of this seemingly modest scene becomes apparent. Toles's evaluation of this and other scenes in Eternal Sunshine allows for an appreciation of how, as viewers, we can benefit and grow from repeated exposure to this film. Pointing out the Nietzschean theme of recurrence in the film that is also explored by Jollimore, Toles draws an insightful analogy between the cycle of repetition in the film and an often overlooked but aesthetically vital feature of film itself: we can (and increasingly do) come back to a film and re-enter the cinematic world offered to us, assured of a perfect fidelity in repetition. He spends some time teasing out this and related features of the phenomenology of film perception, and suggests that one reason Eternal Sunshine haunts us is because its fragmented and cyclical structure, combined with the focus on the fragility of memory, self-consciously invites the viewer to contemplate the intricate assumptions and expectations we bring to the re-viewing of this (and any) film.

There's much more to Toles's essay than this sketch can suggest. He goes on to discuss the too-often-neglected risks that come with "respecting" otherness, as well as the ways in which we regrettably avoid trusting the sometimes opaque but crucial vision provided by love in favor of the clear-cut material effects of power and supposed objectivity of cool detachment. These reflections never stray far from a continual investigation of the relevance of memory to both the film and our lives. Ending with a meditation on the importance to him of his own memories of his parents, Toles provides an examination of Eternal Sunshine that, like the film itself, combines moments of beauty and dramatic force with edifying philosophical insight.[3]

Notes

1 Carroll 2008.
2 Michel Gondry speaking on the commentary to Eternal Sunshine of the Spotless Mind on the movie's DVD.
3 I would like to thank the contributors to this volume as well as Carlene Bauer, Daniel Callcut, Tom Wartenberg, and Susan Watson for helpful feedback on earlier drafts of this introduction.

Reference

Carroll, Noël (2008) "Talk to Them: An Introduction," in A. W. Eaton (ed.) Talk to Her, London and New York: Routledge, pp. 1–10.

Further reading

Cavell, S. (1981) *Pursuits of Happiness: The Hollywood Comedy of Remarriage*, Cambridge, MA: Harvard University Press. (An influential philosophical examination of seven classic romantic comedies in which couples separate only to later reunite.)

Grau, C. (2006) "*Eternal Sunshine of the Spotless Mind* and the Morality of Memory," *Journal of Aesthetics and Art Criticism*, 64:1, 119–133. (A discussion of the ethical issues raised by the memory-erasure process in the film.)

Kaufman, C. (2004) *Eternal Sunshine of the Spotless Mind: The Shooting Script*, New York: Newmarket Press. (In addition to offering the complete shooting script this volume includes an introduction by Michel Gondry and an illuminating interview with Charlie Kaufman.)

Liao, S. M. and Sandberg, A. (2008) "The Normativity of Memory Modification," *Neuroethics*, 1:2, 85–99. (A consideration of the ethical dimensions of current research into developing memory-modifying technologies.)

Margalit, A. *The Ethics of Memory*, Boston, MA: Harvard University Press, 2002. (A comprehensive discussion of the ethical importance of memory, focusing in particular on the question of a community's obligation to maintain collective memories.)

Meyer, M. J. (2008) "Reflections on Comic Reconciliations: Ethics, Memory, and Anxious Happy Endings," *Journal of Aesthetics and Art Criticism*, 66:1, 77–87. (Offers a discussion of *Eternal Sunshine* in the context of the "comedies of remarriage" genre made famous by Cavell.)

Nietzsche, F. (1974) *The Gay Science*, New York: Random House. (Contains Neitzsche's discussion of the idea of eternal recurrence, a notion considered in relation to *Eternal Sunshine* by both Jollimore and Toles in this volume.)

Wartenberg, T. (2007) "Arguing against utilitarianism: *Eternal Sunshine of the Spotless Mind*," in *Thinking on Screen: Film as Philosophy*, New York: Routledge. (A chapter in which Wartenberg makes the case that *Eternal Sunshine* "does" philosophy through offering philosophical arguments.)

Chapter 2

C. D. C. Reeve

TWO BLUE RUINS: LOVE AND MEMORY IN *ETERNAL SUNSHINE OF THE SPOTLESS MIND*

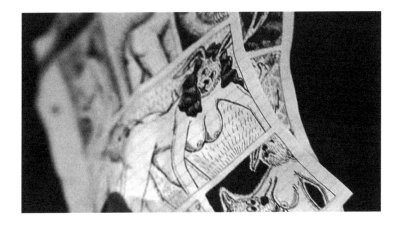

L OVE AIN'T OVER TILL IT'S OVER . . . and it ain't over then,
either. When our lover has gone for good, there are still memories
to haunt us, still mourning to be done, as hard and harrowing as for the
dead. If only we could short-circuit the whole grim process. It's with
that wish that Lacuna, Inc. enters the picture. Plug your brain into its
memory eraser, give the technicians the information they need to target

the right memories, and before you know it the damned spot will be out. "To let people begin again," gushes Mary Svevo (Kirsten Dunst), the adoring secretary of Howard Mierzwiak, Lacuna's guru, "it's beautiful." True, when Mary discovers that her own memories of her love affair with Howard have been erased, her tune changes. "I have since decided that this is horrible . . .," she says. But then, by the time she makes the discovery, her love has re-asserted itself. Watching Howard at his erasing work, she recites the lines of Alexander Pope that provide the film's title, kisses him, and says "I've loved you for a very long time." The roots of her love lie so much deeper than Lacuna's machines can reach, it seems, that erasing her memories, far from destroying her love, leaves it intact but somehow cursed—doomed in its unawareness of the past always to lead to the same awful nowhere. The depth of love, indeed, is pretty much the film's central theme.

Unaware, after receiving the Lacuna treatment, that he has been having a relationship with her for the past two years, Joel Barish (Jim Carrey) meets Clementine Kruczynski (Kate Winslet) at Montauk. "Why," he confides to his journal as he sees her looking at him in the coffee shop, "do I fall in love with every woman I see who shows me the least bit of attention?" One answer, the film suggests, lies, like so many of love's answers, in childhood: "She's not looking at me," Joel's childhood self says of his mother, as his adult self visualizes a childhood scene, "No one ever looks at me." A little later, that same childhood self says, "I want her to pick me up." Then the adult self, as if experiencing the desire all over again, comments, "It's weird how strong that desire is." Joel's loving response to any woman's attention, in other words, was formed early. He has fallen in love with Clementine before. But even when he fell in love with her the first time, during their initial meeting in Montauk, he was repeating himself, falling again in ways he had already fallen long ago. That's one reason Clementine can so readily be assigned roles in his childhood memories, whether as his mother's friend Mrs Hamlyn or as his own childhood sweetheart.

Soon after the scene in the coffee shop, the couple are on the train back to New York. "Okay if I sit closer?" Clementine asks, making an approach Joel himself is too shy to make. "No jokes about my name," she warns.

JOEL: I don't know any jokes about your name.
CLEMENTINE: Huckleberry Hound?

JOEL: I don't know what that means.
CLEMENTINE: Huckleberry Hound? What are you, nuts?

Though we aren't aware of it yet, the exchange reprises a conversation they had when they first met two years earlier. But then Joel knew a lot more. "One of my favorite things when I was a kid," he said, "was my Huckleberry Hound doll." It isn't only Clementine that has been erased from Joel's memory, we see: a chunk of his childhood is gone too. When Joel returns in memory to his early childhood, he sees himself being bathed by his mother in the kitchen sink. "I love being bathed in the sink," his adult self comments. "Such a feeling of security." Imbuing that idyllic sense of security and well-being, and imbued with it, is the song his mother crooned as she soaped and rinsed—"Clementine." When these associations were intact, the film suggests, they were among the roots of his attraction to Clementine—part of what made even her name seem magical. By having the attraction outlive them, however, it also raises doubts about this idea. Perhaps love's real roots lie somewhere else, somewhere even deeper.

Whatever its roots, Joel's attraction to Clementine is pretty easy to understand at a superficial level. She's so luminously beautiful that Patrick (one of Lacuna's employees) falls for her even when she's unconscious. Her attraction to Joel is much more mysterious. What can she possibly see in dull old him? Part of the answer involves a second doll:

CLEMENTINE: When I was a kid I thought I was ugly. Can't believe I'm crying already. Sometimes I think people don't understand how lonely it is to be a kid. Like you don't matter. So, I'm eight . . . and I have these toys, these dolls. My favorite is this ugly girl doll who I call Clementine. And I keep yelling at her, "You can't be ugly! Be pretty!" It's weird. Like if I could transform her, I would magically change too.

Doubtful about her own attractions, the implication is that Clementine is attracted to unprepossessing partners. At times, it's true, she seems more confident of her worth. "You have no idea," she tells Joel, "how lucky you are that I'm interested in you." But the ugly potato-head dolls that fill her apartment tell a different story—a story that Joel, with his brown hair and clothes and love of the TV and the couch, seems to fit right into.

Though the film doesn't tell us explicitly why Joel's Huckleberry Hound doll was his favorite, it provides some significant clues. Explaining to Mierzwiak why she wants Joel erased, Clementine refers to his "pathetic, wimpy, apologetic smile . . . that sort of wounded puppy shit he does." When Joel hears a tape of this conversation, as the two are driving to his apartment, the description touches a nerve: he makes Clementine get out of the car. In the closing scene of the film, as the two Lacuna-ized lovers finally get back together and accept each other, it is Joel's wounded puppy look, we are shown, that melts Clementine's heart. Huckleberry Hound may be forgotten, but what made Joel love him remains intact. It is when he recalls the episode in which Clementine tells him about her doll, indeed, that his doubts about erasure begin. "Mierzwiak," he begs from inside his imagination, "please let me keep this memory, just this one." It's a case of one doll crying out to another.

Because Clementine told Joel about her doll in a moment of intimate self-disclosure, when Lacuna erased Joel, her memory of her doll—like Joel's memory of his doll—had to go too. "Any association" is Mierzwiak's formula for what to target. Instead of the advertised eternal inner sunshine, however, Clementine finds herself a bewildered stranger in her own mind and home. "I'm lost. I'm scared. I feel like I'm disappearing," she tells Patrick. "My skin's coming off! I'm getting old! Nothing makes any sense to me!" It's as if the loss of a potent childhood memory has resulted in the loss of childhood itself ("I'm getting old") and rendered senseless the world the memory helped sustain (all those potato-head dolls). At the same time, Clementine's insecurity about her appearance remains intact: "Do you think I'm ugly?" she asks when Patrick calls her from Joel's apartment. It is the insecurity that makes her skin the intelligible target of her anxiety. "I'm fucking crawling out of my skin," she says, when her dissatisfaction with Joel reaches a peak.

A relationship is a loom. It weaves lives into one another. Just how much unweaving you would have to do in order to erase all traces of one is unclear. And in that un-clarity, which the film subtly exploits, lie grounds for skepticism about the very possibility of what Lacuna purports to be able to do. Erasing a single traumatic memory is one thing. Destroying all recollection of a one-night stand—that's something heavy drinking or a concussion can accomplish. But erasing a long, intimate relationship and all its associations, no matter how far back or how deep they go . . . what would remain? "A new life" is Mierzwiak's reply. Two blue ruins—two sad wrecks—may be the film's.

At the same time as the film encourages skeptical questions about the possibility of memory erasure, it also encourages such questions about Lacuna, and about what it in particular can do. A prime exhibit here is the low-tech, low-rent appearance of the company, its offices and employees. Would anyone in his right mind go to that place and these people to have something done to his brain? I know. The answer is "Yes." Unhappy people—even happy ones—will believe anything, especially anything that promises a quick fix. Look at how much money we spend each year on potions, pills, and procedures of uncertain provenance and unproven efficacy. But that isn't the film's main message. What it seems intent on getting across is that Lacuna is some sort of snake oil.

Patrick is looting the torn-out pages of Joel's journal, purloined from his Lacuna file, for pointers on how to seduce Clementine. A loser with women, he needs all the help he can get. When she suggests that a visit to the frozen Charles River might help put her skin back on, Patrick knows what to do. While she is getting ready, he is looking for the key passage: "Charles. Come on, Charles. 'Look, you and me on the Charles River. I could die right now, Clem. I'm just happy. I've never felt that before. I'm just exactly where I want . . .'" When Patrick begins to recite the old lines of Joel's out there on the ice, however, instead of swooning, Clementine becomes agitated and upset. "I want to go home," she says, and hurries back to the car. Despite Lacuna's promise, the supposedly erased original continues to reverberate. When Clementine re-finds Joel, moreover, and the two are snuggling on her sofa, sipping their Blue Ruins, it's the Charles that immediately resurfaces: "Joel, you should come up to the Charles River with me sometime. It gets frozen this time of the year." Her love-infused memories of her first trip there with Joel are so strong, it seems, that nothing can threaten them. They can even drive out others that compete with them for emotional space: though it was just the previous night that she was Charles-visiting with Patrick, once Joel is back in the game, Clementine seems wholly oblivious of it. In fact, she seems oblivious of Patrick himself. "I so want what's in your suit," she says (somewhat implausibly), when he visits her at work in Barnes and Noble. Well, not any more.

While the vagaries of Clementine's memories are one indication of the unreliability of Lacuna, another is the operation of the process itself.

Perhaps because of an insufficient power supply, Joel, though supposedly deep in drug-induced sleep, can dimly overhear what Patrick and Stan are saying. That's how he discovers that Patrick is stealing his identity in order to get Clementine. He resists erasure, as a result, not only because he realizes how much he loves Clementine and treasures his memories of her but also because jealousy has given his resistance added impetus. The effect on us, however, is that we see how hit-or-miss the erasing process is. When Patrick tricks with the wiring to increase power, Stan says: "Let's not roach the guy." Between being roached and not being deeply enough erased, we are made aware, there is a lot of wiggle room.

While his memories are being given the Lacuna treatment, Joel re-experiences them, in effect conducting a review of his relationship. He remembers good things, such as learning about Clementine's doll and the visit to the frozen Charles. But he also remembers plenty of problems. Some of these were about intimacy and sharing:

> CLEMENTINE: You don't tell me things, Joel. I'm an open book. I tell you everything. Every damn embarrassing thing. You don't trust me . . . People have to share things, Joel . . . That's what intimacy is . . . I wanna read some of those journals you're constantly scribbling in. What do you write in there if you don't have any thoughts or passions . . . or love?

Others had to do with children and commitment. Clementine is ready for both, sure of her competence as a mother. Joel is less sure: "do you really think you could take care of a kid?" Though these are the sorts of problems any young couple might have, in scene after scene we are made aware that Joel and Clementine don't handle them well.

Still angry after the exchange about children and maternal competence, Clementine storms off alone to a party, leaving Joel to stew in his own juices. When she gets home at 3 a.m., "a little tipsy," as she puts it, he is sitting up pretending to read, anxious and angry himself. "I kinda, sorta wrecked your car," she says, in a boozy overstatement. Provoked by Joel's ensuing sermon on drinking and driving, which she rightly diagnoses as displacement behavior, she strikes back: "Face it Joely. You're freaked out because I was out late without you and in your little wormy brain you're trying to figure out, did she fuck someone tonight?" She has hit the nail so painfully on the head that retaliation is immediate and cruel:

"No, see, Clem, I assume you fucked someone tonight. Isn't that how you get people to like you?" He is as aware of her anxieties, after all, as she of his ("if she'll fuck a loser like me, she'll fuck anyone"). That's one of the things intimate disclosure does for you—it arms you with powerful weapons. Though Joel immediately regrets having used them, he has gone too far. Clementine gives him back his apartment keys, walks out, and hires Lacuna. "It would be different," Joel imagines Clementine telling him a little later, "if we could just give it another go round." It's a consoling thought, no doubt, and not an uncommon one to have when a relationship ends. But why believe that, in this case, it has any basis in reality? Why believe that Joel and Clementine wouldn't in fact behave in just the same old ways?

Disillusioned with Howard, Mary has sent his patients their files, including tapes of their pre-erasure conversations with him. "We've met," she says in an accompanying note, "but you don't remember me."[1] When Joel and Clementine get back from their picnic on the Charles, the tapes are in their mailboxes. When they listen to Clementine's in the car, it seems like "some sort of teaser ad." Then Joel thinks that Clementine is somehow screwing with him and makes her get out. Eventually, however, they come to realize that the other go round they wished for is actually in progress. As Clementine joins Joel in his apartment to talk over what this implies, his tape is playing: "The only way Clem thinks she can get people to like her is to fuck 'em . . . or at least dangle the possibility of being fucked in front of 'em." Again, her reaction is to leave: "I'm a little confused. I don't really think I can be here." After erasure, we are reminded, whatever explains her behavior is still intact, doing the same fast work of cutting off painful contact.

Though we seem to be in for a real break-up this time, like the one between Mary and Howard, we also know the film is unlikely to let that happen. And, sure enough, after a few tense moments, there is a change in the pattern. Joel follows her into the corridor. "I want you to wait for a while," he says, his face all wounded puppy. By finding what it takes to keep Clementine in contact with him for those few extra seconds, he has enabled that look to work its anxiety-quieting magic:

> CLEMENTINE: I'm not a concept, Joel, I'm just a fucked-up girl who's looking for my own peace of mind. I'm not perfect.

JOEL: I can't see anything that I don't like about you. Right now I can't.

CLEMENTINE: But you will. But you will, you know. You know you will think of things, and I'll get bored with you and feel trapped because that's what happens with me.

JOEL: Okay.

CLEMENTINE: Okay. Okay.

JOEL: Okay. (*They begin to laugh.*)

As we cut to a scene of the two lovers playing on snowy Montauk beach, we hear Beck singing "Change your heart . . .". It is a foretaste of the sunny-snowy, good-bad tomorrows that changed hearts make possible.

In the case of Clementine, what caused the change is, in a way, nothing. She already has the sort of heart that Joel, through suffering, must acquire. Capable of intimate disclosure, eager to have children, able to understand that lovers must learn to take the bad with the good, she is already an adult, already aware of what she's like. "You know me," she says to explain why she hired Lacuna, "I'm impulsive." She also knows the illusions men have about her and warns Joel about them when he asks her out for the first time: "Look man, I'm telling you right off the bat, I'm high maintenance . . . Too many guys think I'm a concept, or I complete them, or I'm gonna make them alive. But I'm just a fucked-up girl looking for my own peace of mind. Don't assign me yours." When she repeats part of this warning in the closing scene, we see how old the wisdom is. Nonetheless, as Joel admits to her in his imaginary recapitulation of the scene, it was a warning he didn't take: "I still thought you were going to save my life, even after that."

The phrases "make them alive" and "save my life" are potent ones, which are made all the more so by the visual meaning the film assigns to them: the dull colors Joel favors seem like vampires sucking droplets of vitality from Clementine's bright and often ravishingly beautiful ones. "I think if there's a truly seductive quality about Clementine," he says to Mierzwiak, "it's that her personality promises to take you out of the mundane . . . into another world where things are exciting." He's not whistling Dixie. And the film lets us see that. "I need your lovin'," Beck sings, "like the sunshine." The first time around, that's how Joel needs Clementine's loving—something to warm and excite him and give him life. As he imaginatively reviews his relationship with her, though, she becomes something else, something that can help him overcome his anxieties and do some living and shining of his own.

Like any such review, Joel's is a work of memory and imagination. But Clementine, we are shown, is as much herself in the other as in the one—as uncannily autonomous in Joel's fantasies as she is in his memories of reality. While it is no doubt difficult to explain just what that means or how it is possible, it is a perfectly familiar phenomenon. We know much more about our lovers than we can possibly articulate. When we stage fantasy scenes involving them, something we are endlessly doing, this inarticulate knowledge influences what we can make them say or do. We might want to fantasize about them catering to our wishes in ways they don't, but when we try, we often find that the fantasy falls apart or lacks credibility or goes off in unwanted directions. Like characters in good novels, our lovers have lives of their own, even inside us, which is why we can learn about them from our fantasies: when we see what we can or can't convincingly make them do, knowledge that was inarticulate acquires a voice, a look, a definition. It is one of the minor triumphs of the film that it is so aware of this and finds such a compelling way of communicating it.

The chief role Joel assigns to Clementine in his fantasies is that of an agent of resistance to her own erasure. It's a brilliant conceit, which allows self-examination and psychological working through to take on the excitement of a chase sequence. The first hurdle she must help him surmount is his apparently helpless condition. He is asleep, trapped in Lacuna's (however inept) clutches. "Wake yourself up," she tells him. Despite his skepticism, the idea works to some extent. By making an effort, he does wake up for a moment. (It's a small allegory of his life.) More significant successes soon arrive: "Joel, the eraser guys are coming here, so what if you take me somewhere else, somewhere where I don't belong, and we hide there till morning?" This idea is so clever that it stumps Stan, who has been too busy fooling around and getting stoned with Mary to keep an eye on what's happening in Joel's brain: "It stopped erasing. Oh, shit! This is terrible. He's off the map." Within minutes— very funny minutes—Stan is calling Howard for help: "I'm working on this guy, down here, and we seem to have lost him for a moment, and, uh, I can't . . . I can't bring him back up." The place Joel has thought to hide Clementine is his childhood—an area in his brain that is outside the one Lacuna has mapped for treatment.

In the subsequent scenes set there, Joel and Clementine appear as themselves, as miniature versions of themselves, as their childhood selves, and, in Clementine's case, as Mrs Hamlyn and Joel's childhood sweetheart. Though it isn't always easy to see why they switch roles when they do, the message is plain enough: Joel's childhood contains avatars of Clementine; his adult relationship with her, infantile residues. What the scenes constitute, as a result, is the sort of imaginative work that can transform anxieties. One of these, as we saw, concerns Clementine's capacities as a mother. Correlated with it is the following scene in which Joel experiences her effective mothering of his own childhood self:

> JOEL: Ice-cream!
> CLEMENTINE (*as Mrs. Hamlyn*): No, not until after, you know, you've had your dinner. (*To adult Joel*) Come on, Joel. Joel, grow up!
> JOEL (*adult*): Don't leave me, Clem. Oh, my God, Clem.
> CLEMENTINE (*as her adult self*): This is sort of warped.
> JOEL (*miniature, childhood self*): I'm scared. I want my mommy.
> CLEMENTINE (*as Mrs. Hamlyn*): Don't cry, baby Joel. Baby Joel, it's okay. (*As her adult self to the adult Joel*) Joel. Joely. Joel! Stop it! Look, I think it's working. Look, we're hidden, Joel. Look! Hey honey, look. Wait there (*she lifts up her skirt to reveal her panties*). My crotch is still here, just as you remembered it.
> JOEL: Yuck!

As Clementine switches backwards and forwards between being baby Joel's mother and adult Joel's lover an equivalence is established between the lover's ingenuity in preserving an adult relationship from erasure and the mother's ability to stay in a reassuring relationship with an anxious and needy child, who must sometimes be given what he wants, sometimes not. Despite the "Yuck!" baby Joel's gaze remains riveted—even if he doesn't yet quite know why.

Safe until Howard appears on the scene, Joel's early childhood is soon a place the lovers have to flee. But where? Again, the suggestion comes from the ever-resourceful Clementine. If Joel had anxieties about her suitability as a partner—and he did—his own imagination is proving them groundless. "Hide me in your humiliation," she says. The word is no sooner uttered than it triggers a memory. A page of Joel's pornographic drawings fills the screen. A naked man with a dog's head is licking the genitals of a dog-headed woman with large breasts. His Huckleberry Hound doll has become an adolescent. As the page begins rhythmically moving, we see that Joel (as his adult rather than his adolescent self) is masturbating while holding it in his lap. At first, Clementine, who (as her adult self) is in bed beside him, turns away in disgust. "I don't like it either," he responds. "I'm just trying to find horrible secret places to . . . ." Suddenly, the bedroom door opens. It's his mother. When she sees what he's doing, she takes it in stride: "Oh, um, uh, you know what honey? I'm just gonna ask you in the morning. Goodnight sweetheart!" Though Clementine laughs as Joel covers his head with the bedclothes, she is soon loving and reassuring. His sexual needs, however humiliating to reveal or admit, are safe with her (as safe, apparently, as with his own remarkably broad-minded and sensitive mother!).

Watching for brain activity on his computer screen, Howard is soon blipping away again, forcing the lovers to move on to "somewhere really buried," as Clementine puts it. The result is an imaginative re-staging of an elaborate scene in which Joel's childhood self, attired in a red cape (which alternates with a similarly attired version of his adult self), is being dared by a group of young boys to hit a dead bird with a hammer. "Hit it! Hit it!" they chant. "Come on, you big sissy!" Unable to withstand their taunting, Joel smashes the bird to a bloody pulp and bursts into tears. As a live bird that has been watching from a treetop flies off, Joel's childhood sweetheart (who alternates with miniature Clementine) steps in, grabs his hand, and begins to lead him away:

> FREDDY (*one of the boys*): Ooh! Ooh! He has a girlfriend!
> JOEL (*as his adult self*): Wait. What am I doing? You know something, Freddy?
> FREDDY: And he loves her!
> JOEL: You don't scare me anymore.

What begins in memory ends in fantasy: it's the adult not the childhood Joel who isn't scared and returns to fight Freddy. When Freddy easily wins even then, we see that fantasy can only accomplish so much. Again, Clementine is needed to save the day: "Joel! Joely! Get up. Come on, it's not worth it." As the two walk off, alternating their child-adult roles, we hear Joel's adult voice say "I'm so ashamed" and Clementine respond "It's okay. You were a little kid."

If this were a movie by Andrei Tarkovsky or Krzysztof Kieslowski, a scene so apparently rich in symbolism might merit and reward detailed analysis. I'm not sure that the same holds here. What we are to take away, I suspect, is simply that Joel's adult timidity has childhood roots. He was a gentle little boy, who could not stand up for gentleness in the face of bullying—or for himself. The shame that he has so resolutely hidden seems to be as much about the one as the other: he isn't strong enough either to be gentle or to be strong.

In the shooting script, Clementine seems squarely on the side of that shame. She wants a man not a wimp:

> CLEMENTINE (*to Mierzwiak on tape*): Is it so much to ask for an actual man to have sex with? . . . I might as well be a lesbian. At least I could have someone pretty to look at while I'm fucking. Not that we fuck anymore. I mean, I don't call it fucking on the rare occasions that it happens. Not fucking . . . *faking*. Honey, let's *fake* tonight. Make a few faces, get it over with. Shit . . . I remember this time I made him come out onto this frozen river with me. He was terrified. Like a goddamn girl . . . Ugh.[2]

While this critique is dimly memorialized in the film—most explicitly in a few epithets she applies to Joel, of which "faggot" and "old lady" are the most pointed—Clementine herself has decisively switched sides. Instead of wanting a strong, phallic male, she now seems positively to relish Joel's insecure, timid, sexlessness. In his fantasies, she's the one with the balls. In her reality, that now seems hunky-dory. He'll be the girl, she the man.

The final episode Joel remembers from his childhood, though included under the rubric of his humiliation, is perhaps best seen as a coda to the one we've just been discussing. Arriving outside Joel's childhood home, the two begin to play a game in which Clementine lies on the grass, while Joel straddles her and smothers her with a pillow. The point of the game is to try to scare the smotherer into thinking he has really killed you by playing dead when he lifts the pillow. The point of the *scene*, on the other hand, seems to be to drive home once again that adult sexual life is a reprise of childhood—the child, father to the man.

Mid-game, Howard again discovers the location of the fleeing lovers—"I think I got the hang of this. I still don't understand it, but I'm finding him quickly enough." As his fingers click the keys, Joel's house loses definition and begins to fade. The raised pillow reveals nothing but grass: Clementine is gone. Faster than Howard's fingers, however, are Joel's synapses and the association the game has triggered. What he remembers is playing the same game on his couch with the adult Clementine. As she presses the pillow on his face, he gropes her breasts and buttocks. The incipient little death of adulthood has replaced the pretend big one of childhood. It's about as sexual as the film allows their relationship to get.

When Joel remembers his first meeting with Clementine, the same point about adulthood as a reprise of childhood is made again in a much more freighted context. The two are walking on Montauk beach in the late evening. They arrive at a beautiful empty beach house. As they go up the steps to explore it, they begin to talk. Clementine quickly discovers that Joel is unmarried and straight. Then, to his consternation, already awakened by the question about his sexual orientation, she proceeds to do a little housebreaking. Reluctantly, he joins her, as afraid as he was (both times) to walk on the icy Charles.

> JOEL: I think we should go.
> CLEMENTINE: Why? It's our house just for tonight. We are—(*she looks at some mail*)—David and Ruth Laskin. Which one do you want to be?
> JOEL: Uh?
> CLEMENTINE: I prefer to be Ruth, but I can be flexible.

It's a prefiguring of what their actual relationship will end up being like, with their gender roles, as we saw, (satisfyingly) reversed. Then, leaving Joel to choose a wine from the liquor cabinet she has found, Clementine heads upstairs to "slip into something more Ruth." But it's all too much for him: "I really should go. I've gotta catch my ride." For Clementine too, it seems, it's the last straw: "So go," she replies.

We feel—and are intended to feel—some of Clementine's frustration at having found so limp a guy. But before that feeling can congeal, Joel's elaboration of the remembered scene in his imagination is under way. In it, both agree that they wish he had stayed. So why didn't he?

> JOEL: I don't know. I felt like a scared little kid. I was like—it was above my head. I don't know.
> CLEMENTINE: You were scared?

> JOEL: Yeah. Thought you knew that about me. I ran back to the
> bonfire trying to outrun my humiliation, I think.
> CLEMENTINE: Was it something I said?
> JOEL: Yeah. You said "So go" with such disdain.

The great circle that opened that day in childhood with Freddy and the battered bird has closed. The disdain Joel hears isn't in Clementine's voice, if we listen; it is an echo of the past. Frustration somehow no longer seems the appropriate reaction—anyway, not on our part.

If Joel could remember these scenes when he gets his second chance with Clementine, they would surely help him handle the anxieties about intimacy and commitment that helped ruin their relationship. Having done all that imaginative work to such reassuring effect, he should be better able to do it in reality. Howard's confident "Okay" as he closes his laptop and leaves Joel's apartment seems to preclude that possibility. But the skepticism we have been encouraged to have about Lacuna, and about Howard himself, is there as an antidote. As Joel drives Clementine to his apartment after their (second) night on the Charles, they have a brief conversation before the fateful tape begins to play:

> JOEL: I . . . I had a really nice time last night.
> CLEMENTINE: Nice?
> JOEL: I had the best fucking night of my entire fucking life last night!
> CLEMENTINE: That's better. (*She opens Mary's letter.*)

She's right. It *is* better—better than ever. Howard notwithstanding, Joel's long inner night-ride is paying dividends. In the final scene, as we saw, it seems to save the relationship.

Thus far we are in the real world—a world of cause and effect and of the long shadows childhood casts. A world the film, too, largely inhabits. Memory erasure is part of that world. Amnesia is science, so to speak, not science fiction. Lacuna, if not already in a storefront near you, has analogues that are not so far away from a local medical school. Treatments for post-traumatic stress already in development may well give new meaning to the phrase "morning-after pill." At the same time, however, the film also disconcertingly dips into another world—a world, like that of our dreams, where true lovers find and re-find one another in flagrant violation of causation and the other laws by which reality is constrained.

When Clementine and Patrick are driving back from their abortive trip to the Charles, they too have a brief conversation. When he tells her she's "nice," she is outraged and *we* know why. We have heard her being "nice"-ed to death by Joel on the train back from Montauk: "Oh, God! Don't you know any other adjectives? I don't need 'nice.' I don't need myself to be it, and I don't need anybody else to be it to me." The problem is that that event is in Clementine's *future* when she reacts to Patrick. So unless the film is playing with backwards causation, it has slipped into a fantasy world.

This is a minor example, admittedly, and if it were the only one, we might be inclined to write it off as sloppy editing or a false step. But there is another that is so crucial to the film's plot that it cannot be treated so cavalierly. As Joel imaginatively elaborates on the scene of his humiliation in the beach house, Clementine comes up with her final suggestion for how to outwit Lacuna. "Meet me in Montauk," she whispers. It's just possible that Joel's synapses are once again faster than Howard's fingers and that Clementine's suggestion doesn't get erased until after it has had its effect. When Joel wakes up the next morning, therefore, it is with the unconscious intention to go to Montauk that the suggestion has planted. But that, of course, would not explain why Clementine goes there, let alone why her visit is coordinate with his. When Joel, from inside his imagination, wants to call things off, Mierzwiak replies: "I'm part of your imagination too, Joel, how can I help you from there?" What goes for him goes for Clementine. As a part of Joel's imagination, she is in no position to form intentions for the real Clementine to execute.

True, we don't absolutely *have* to believe in the mysterious double efficacy of Clementine's suggestion for the plot to work. Coincidences happen. But the feeling the film creates is of inevitability, not happenstance. Joel and Clementine, it tells us, *had* to meet in Montauk. Perhaps it produces this feeling by flirting with the paranormal—with fate, or kismet, or some muddled version of Nietzschean eternal return. Perhaps its message is that love's roots lie too deep for science, because they lie outside the reality that is science's theater of operations. But since the film is, in other regards, so sensible, it may be that all it really does is seduce *us*—to the extent we need Joel and Clementine to get back together—into doing some illicitly deep digging of our own. Wishful thinking, notoriously, is magical thinking.

Though Eternal Sunshine seems to invite philosophical thought primarily about memory erasure, such philosophical thinking as it does itself seems to have more to do with love and its essential involvement with the past—particularly with the childhood past. Erase the memories of our lovers, it shows us, and with them go our childhood dolls, our mother's bathtime songs, our very sense of what security and happiness might consist in. Deprived of all that, what would we have to love with? What would we have to give in intimate exchange? Who, erotically, would we be? In a million films, the hard-faced men pursue, the lovers run for their lives. In this one, the men's faces are softer, but the stakes are just as high. It is their love lives, we are shown, that Joel and Clementine are running for.

Notes

1 Are we meant to notice the tension between this claim and her comment on the phone to Mrs Sobel, a repeat customer, that she "can't have the procedure done three times in one month"?
2 Kaufman 2004, pp. 121–2.

References

Kaufman, Charlie (2004) Eternal Sunshine of the Spotless Mind: The Shooting Script, New York: Newmarket Press.

Chapter 3

Troy Jollimore

MISERABLY EVER AFTER: FORGETTING, REPEATING AND AFFIRMING LOVE IN *ETERNAL SUNSHINE OF THE SPOTLESS MIND*

> To be incapable of taking one's enemies, one's accidents, even one's misdeeds seriously for very long—that is the sign of strong, full natures in whom there is an excess of the power to form, to mold, to recuperate, and to forget.
>
> Friedrich Nietzsche[1]

Deciding to remember, and what to remember, is how we decide who
we are.

Robert Pinsky[2]

Introduction

BOY MEETS GIRL. Boy loses memory. Boy meets girl. Put in such
a tidy nutshell, the plot of Michel Gondry and Charlie Kaufmann's
Eternal Sunshine of the Spotless Mind might seem fairly straightforward. But the
philosophical issues raised by this intriguing story—the story of two
people who try to put the past behind them by having their memories
of each other erased, and only end up repeating the very relationship they
were trying to put behind them—are anything but straightforward. In
this paper I want to explore some of those issues, and the interrelations
between them, particularly as they connect to three central themes:
memory, affirmation, and repetition.

Start with repetition. From a certain point of view, *Eternal Sunshine of the
Spotless Mind* is one of the few films one can recall that leaves its main
characters almost exactly where it finds them: a pair of near-strangers in
the very early stages of what is likely to be a difficult, indeed tumultuous,
romantic relationship. Yet this summary again risks making the situation
of the lovers seem more straightforward than it actually is. After all, if at
the end of the film Joel Barish and Clementine Kruczynski are in a sense
strangers to each other, it is at the same time true not only that they have
known each other intimately but that they know (thanks to their own
brutally honest recorded comments) a great deal about each other. And
if, at the start, they think it *likely* that their relationship will be a trying
one, at the end of the film they are in a position to be very nearly certain
that this is the case. And this is an important difference.

Indeed, the idea of beginning a relationship under such conditions
may seem both absurd and hopeless. For surely there is a certain level of
ignorance that is necessary at the start of a love affair. Perhaps the
idealization of one's beloved is a necessary part of infatuation. Perhaps,
too, it is necessary to pass through the infatuation stage in order to develop
a commitment strong enough to weather the difficulties that will present
themselves as one goes on to develop a more accurate and more realistic
picture of the person to whom one is committed. One is reminded of
Charlotte's claim, in *Pride and Prejudice*, that at least at the beginning of a

relationship "it is better to know as little as possible of the defects of the person with whom you are to pass your life"—a species of ignorance that is entirely unavailable to Joel and Clementine at *Eternal Sunshine's* conclusion.[3]

Although their desire, in seeking out the services of Lacuna, Inc. (the company that performs the memory erasure), is to be liberated from a painful past, it might be suggested that in purging their memories of one another, Joel and Clementine are only setting themselves up for a second round of pain and despair. "If one has character," writes Nietzsche, "one also has one's typical experience, which occurs repeatedly."[4] In reliving their experience of meeting, loving, and despairing, this couple becomes living proof of George Santayana's maxim that "those who cannot remember the past are condemned to repeat it"[5]—and become, at the same time, living counter-examples to Nietzsche's dictum, "Blessed are the forgetful, for they get the better even of their blunders."[6] That line from Nietzsche is, of course, quoted as a line of dialogue in *Eternal Sunshine*. The quoter is Mary Svevo, a Lacuna employee who, as it turns out, is dragging her own submerged history behind her (and who will ultimately be responsible for Joel and Clementine's finding out the truth). Mary has not made a systematic reading of Nietzsche; she only knows this quotation because, as she puts it, "[I] found it in my *Bartlett's*." Her knowledge of Nietzsche is as incomplete, in fact, as her knowledge of her own past. She is thus not aware that Nietzsche's thinking about forgetfulness is far more complex and ambivalent than this simple quotation suggests.

My interest in Nietzsche, for the purposes of this paper, lies not only in his profound insights regarding memory and forgetfulness but also in the fact that one of the deep issues that troubled him throughout his philosophical career was the issue of affirmation. Indeed it is perhaps no exaggeration to say that the question of how to endorse, how to say yes to, the nature and value of human existence—to recognize a human life as a life worth living even in the light of all we know about its flaws and limitations—was the central philosophical question for Nietzsche. And the idea of affirmation is central to the positive conceptions he put forward, not only in response to the question of how one ought to philosophize but also in response to the question of how one ought to live:

We others, we immoralists, have, conversely, made room in our hearts for every kind of understanding, comprehending, and approving. We do not easily negate; we make it a point of honor to be affirmers.[7]

In *Eternal Sunshine of the Spotless Mind*, Joel and Clementine are faced with their own versions of the question of affirmation. How, in the wake of a failed love relationship, does one manage to move on and say yes to the possibility of love? And is it possible, at the outset of what one knows will be a doomed relationship, to nonetheless affirm the possibility of love in a way that allows one to proceed? The answers these two characters provide vary greatly throughout the course of the film. In this paper I will attempt to interpret these answers in connection with a number of Nietzschean theses about affirmation. Ultimately I want to suggest that *Eternal Sunshine* can be read as the story of two persons who learn to be "immoralists" in Nietzsche's sense: who learn, that is, to refuse to negate, to "make it a point of honor to be affirmers."

"To let people begin again": The value of forgetting

You must learn some of my philosophy.—Think only of the past as its remembrance gives you pleasure.

Elizabeth Bennett, in *Pride and Prejudice*[8]

The human individual remembers many of her experiences but forgets a great many more; and what is remembered is remembered only partially, incompletely, and frequently inaccurately. It is natural to see this tendency to forget as a weakness, an unfortunate consequence of the fact that our cognitive abilities are finite. One of Nietzsche's great insights—an insight that was picked up and greatly elaborated upon by Freud—was to suggest that we might instead view the ability to forget as a cognitive *achievement*, an ability that humans need to develop in order to survive and flourish. "Forgetting is no mere *vis inertiae* as the superficial imagine," Nietzsche writes. "It is rather an active and in the strictest sense positive faculty of repression."[9]

This view of forgetting is part and parcel of Nietzsche's larger view of human cognition. Nietzsche saw himself as supplying a corrective, and indeed a rebuke, to the Enlightenment view that tended to place an unconditional value on knowledge, and to assume that it was always better to come to know more. Nietzsche was among the first philosophers to take seriously the thought that *too much* knowledge could be a hindrance rather than a boon. He found—as he so often managed to do—a particularly provocative way of putting the point: in terms of what he called a *will to ignorance*:

> It is not enough that you understand in what ignorance humans as well as animals live; you must also have and acquire the *will* to ignorance. You need to grasp that without this kind of ignorance life itself would be impossible, that it is a condition under which alone the living thing can preserve itself and prosper: a great, firm dome of ignorance must encompass you.[10]

Why, exactly, did Nietzsche accept the necessity of the will to ignorance? There is no simple answer to this question. Sometimes what Nietzsche seems to have in mind is the thought that the world is *complex*: so complex that we must simplify it in order to function adequately within it. This view might be combined with a view about the finitude of human capacities. The suggestion would then be that since a human agent will never be able to complete the process of forming a comprehensive detailed picture of the world, it is a mistake to wait around until such a picture is arrived at; the result of doing so would be paralysis. Moreover, if we share Nietzsche's view that human identity is itself a kind of fiction that we project onto the world, then we will be likely to agree with him that a person who cannot *forget* that she is a fiction will be unable to participate in ordinary human life. One who "does not possess the power to forget," writes Nietzsche in his *Unfashionable Observations*, would be "damned to see becoming everywhere." Ultimately such a person:

> would no longer believe in his own being, would no longer believe in himself, would see everything flow apart in turbulent particles, and would lose himself in this stream of becoming; like the true student of Heraclitus, in the end he would hardly even dare to lift a finger. All action requires forgetting[.][11]

A related but distinct version of the point abandons the appeal to human finitude and instead holds that a genuinely comprehensive cognitive grasp of the world is problematic, not (merely) because it is practically inaccessible to us but because even if it were accessible, it would not be helpful. The world, that is, is so alien, so inherently resistant to being understood in human terms, and perhaps so pervasively self-contradictory that a true picture of it would not assist us in responding to it; indeed, by revealing that there is no such thing as an appropriate or adequate response, such an understanding would actually make it impossible to act. On this understanding the "will to ignorance" is necessary not because the world is too complex for us to grasp but because it is in itself meaningless. Humans can only find meaning in the world by imposing meaning upon it, and the imposing of meaning is, in part, a matter of selective cognition: we perceive (that is, incorporate into our under-standings) the parts of the world that are compatible with our own conceptions of its meaning, and suppress or ignore the rest.

Finally, a further interpretation suggests that the world is not only *meaningless* but positively *bad*: if we truly grasped the desperate nature of our plight, we would be too demoralized to act. To take what is perhaps the most obvious example, one might well think that a person who cannot ever *forget* that he is mortal and therefore doomed to death and the ultimate erasure of all his accomplishments would in all likelihood be too depressed to strive to achieve anything at all. Similarly, a person who cannot forget her failures, errors and other assorted sources of shame and regret may be so overcome with them that she will find herself unable to go on with life and try anything new. "The man in whom this apparatus of repression is damaged and ceases to function properly," Nietzsche writes, "may be compared (and more than merely compared) with a dyspeptic—he cannot 'have done' with anything."[12] In *Beyond Good and Evil* he describes the process aphoristically:

> "I have done that," says my memory. "I cannot have done that," says my pride, and remains inexorable. Eventually—memory yields.[13]

It is the third version of the case for 'active forgetting' that seems most pertinent to the situation of Joel and Clementine. Their problem does not seem to be that the world is *complex*, nor even that it is *meaningless*; rather, they suffer from the fact that the world—more precisely, the recent past —is *bad*. They are burdened with the psychic scars of a failed relation-ship in a way that causes them great pain and makes it difficult for them to move on. Their wish, then, is to return to the ideal (or perhaps idealized) state of existence they experienced prior to the onset of the relationship.

Indeed, on the account provided by Mary Svevo, the return to such an idealized state of being is precisely the point of the procedure:

> It's amazing, isn't it? Such a gift Howard is giving the world. [. . .] To let people begin again. It's beautiful. You look at a baby and it's so fresh, so clean, so free. Adults . . . they're like this mess of anger and phobias and sadness . . . hopelessness. And Howard just makes it go away.[14]

This gives us, then, our first Nietzschean thesis regarding affirmation:

> The First Affirmation Thesis: Affirming the value of one's life, and being able to act positively and decisively in it, requires denying (and where possible, forgetting) those negative aspects that threaten to make such action impossible.

But, one might ask, why does the Lacuna procedure aim to eliminate *all* memories of a relationship? Why not erase only the negative ones? One answer is that memories are so intricately and complexly interwoven that one must purge all memories connected with a given individual or relationship if the procedure is to have any chance of success. Another quite different sort of explanation rests on the fact that in the aftermath of a love affair *all* memories, those of pleasurable experiences as well as those of unpleasant ones, are liable to provoke pain. Memories of negative experiences—feeling unhappy with one's lover, feeling jealous, being hurt by her cutting remarks—will be painful for obvious reasons. But memories of happy experiences will also hurt, for they will serve as reminders of what has been lost. Indeed, a good deal of the pain of lost love stems from the fact that our feelings about the end of love are quite similar to, and may remind us of, our feelings about our own mortality— a set of facts that our faculty of active forgetting must cover up if we are to live successfully.

The end of a love affair is invariably painful. But even while an affair is still going on, love frequently involves as much pain as pleasure. Quite often, indeed, it involves more. As one of the most intense of human experiences, love can involve some of the most intense feelings of fear, guilt, shame, and anxiety that one will ever experience. It seems likely, then, that a willingness to love, particularly in the aftermath of a failed relationship, is largely dependent on one's capacity for active forgetting. For how many of us could bring ourselves, even permit ourselves, to love, if our romantic and utopian idealizations about love came to be replaced by accurate memories of the anxiety, despair, and outright pain that love so frequently engenders?

"The strength of a spirit": Against forgetting

It was as if I had just awakened from a dream that had lasted for years. And suddenly I was afraid and felt a cold sweat form on my body. I was frightened by the terrible strength of man, his desire and ability to forget. I realized I was ready to forget everything, to cross out twenty years of my life. And when I understood this, I conquered myself, I knew I would not permit my memory to forget everything that I had seen. And I regained my calm and fell asleep.

Varlam Shalamov[15]

But perhaps this will seem too despairing. Love, for all its pain, also brings a great deal of happiness, even joy; and while one's feelings about a failed relationship in its immediate aftermath are often dominated by anger and regret, making it impossible to take pleasure even in the most pleasant of the memories that remain, a more benign and pleasant interpretation of that particular segment of one's history frequently comes to dominate with the passage of time. Of course, this process is itself, in large part, an instance of active forgetting. And it is significant that both Joel and Clementine make their decision to have each other artificially erased (engaging in what we might perhaps term "very active forgetting") quickly and impulsively, with little deliberation, soon enough after the end of the relationship that they are still deeply hurt and aggrieved. Moreover Joel, at least, soon comes to regret his decision—not before the erasure (when the pain is still too fresh), nor after (when the pain, along with the memories, have been eliminated), but during the process of erasure.

Why might one come to regret the decision to forget? Nietzsche himself, for all he had to say in favor of forgetting, was ultimately ambivalent on its value. He admitted, as we have seen, that forgetting was *necessary*:

in his view, we could not flourish or even, perhaps, survive without it. Yet to call something necessary is perfectly compatible with regarding it as a necessary evil. Nietzsche's insight into the positive aspects of forgetting is balanced by a recognition that points us in the opposite direction, reminding us that remembering has a value, and that if forgetting is a matter of masking the less palatable aspects of existence in order to be able to live, then a sign of the strong, the powerful, will be that they will not need to forget as much:

> Something might be true while being harmful and dangerous in the highest degree. Indeed, it may be a basic characteristic of existence that those who would know it completely would perish, in which case the strength of a spirit should be measured according to how much of the "truth" one could still barely endure—or, to put it more clearly, to what degree one would *require* it to be thinned down, shrouded, sweetened, blunted, falsified.[16]

This, then, gives us a second Nietzschean thesis regarding affirmation— one whose spirit is quite contrary to that of the first:

> *The Second Affirmation Thesis*: One ought to affirm the individual components of one's life, even when it is painful to do so. Denying reality is a sign of weakness; affirming the unpleasant aspects of the real is a sign of strength.

The thought is that remembering, for all its psychic costs—indeed, *on account of* its psychic costs—might best be seen as a sign of strength, a sign that one can accept, tolerate, and even master the dread realities of life, rather than admitting a kind of defeat by denying them.

The defeat in question is no trivial matter, for what is lost when memories are purged is something quite fundamental. Memories are not just valued *by* or important *to* us—for words such as 'by' and 'to' suggest a view of memories as objects separate from ourselves, to which we bear certain relationships. Rather, it is plausible to think that the relationship between me and my memories is substantially more intimate than that: not a relationship of valuing or significance, but of *identity*. My memories, that is, can plausibly be viewed as parts of me: my remembering (at least some of) the significant experiences of my life is an essential part of my being the person I am.[17] A bout of complete amnesia regarding such matters—one that plunged me into a state in which I was quite literally unable to remember, from the first-point of view, any of my past experiences—would almost certainly result in a very profound crisis of identity. Sacrificing one's memories in order to escape from pain is akin to sacrificing a limb in order to escape from a trap: it is quite literally a portion of oneself that is jettisoned.

By choosing to forget, we are in effect amputating parts of ourselves. And if we forget too much, whether by accident or by choice, we will lose our sense of self, our understanding of who we are. In her story "Almost No Memory" Lydia Davis describes the situation of a person who, while her present-moment consciousness is "very sharp," is unable to form memories of her experiences. She attempts to deal with this, in part, by taking notes on the books she reads; but this strategy only leaves her in a situation of profound uncertainty amounting to a kind of epistemological despair:

> And so she knew by this that these notebooks truly had a great deal to do with her, though it was hard for her to understand, and troubled her to try to understand, just how they had to do with her, how much they were of her and how much they were outside her and not of her, as they sat there on the shelf, being what she knew but did not know, being what she had read but did not remember reading, being what she had thought but did not now think, or remember thinking, or if she remembered, then did not know whether she was thinking it now or whether she had only once thought it, or understand why she had had a thought once and then years later had the same thought, or a thought once and then never that same thought again.[18]

Because the character in Davis's story cannot construct a coherent narrative to fit together the various pieces of evidence she possesses about herself—the books, notes, fragments of persisting memory, etc.—she simply cannot understand herself. These pieces of evidence come to her as if they had been created by someone else. The result is that she is, in a very real sense, isolated from herself. Nor will this isolation extend only as far as the boundaries of her own self—boundaries that, in her case, seem to be in some serious danger of dissolving. It is through our experiences of the world that we gain access to that world; and so it is only to the extent that we are able to continue to possess those experiences by remembering them that we can regard ourselves as having access to the larger world (larger, that is, than the extraordinarily limited portion of it to which our senses provide access at any particular moment). But this larger, public world is precisely the place where we encounter people other than ourselves—a point that has been forcefully made by Harry Frankfurt:

> Lies are designed to damage our grasp of reality. So they are intended, in a very real way, to make us crazy. To the extent that we believe them, our minds are occupied and governed by fictions, fantasies, and illusions that have been concocted for us by the liar. What we accept as real is a world that others cannot see, touch, or experience in any direct way. A person who believes a lie is constrained by it, accordingly, to live "in his own world"—a world that others cannot enter, and in which even the liar himself does not truly reside. Thus, the victim of the lie is, in the degree of his deprivation of the truth, shut off from the world of common experience and isolated in an illusory realm to which there is no path that others might find or follow.[19]

The loss of our experiential memories isolates us not only from ourselves, but from others as well. Joel's and Clementine's mutual friends Rob and Carrie, for instance, are placed in the difficult position of not only having to conceal their knowledge of the relationship from (post-erasure) Clementine but having to conceal their knowledge of Clementine's decision to have him erased from (pre-erasure) Joel. They are thus forced to adopt a kind of paternalistic stance toward both of the former lovers— a stance that, as it turns out, cannot be long maintained: Rob soon breaks and reveals all to the shocked and horrified Joel. Of course it is an interesting fact that, in choosing to respond by having Clementine, in her turn, erased, Joel is deliberately choosing a course in which his friends will need to adopt an even more radically paternalistic stance toward him. But we must once again remind ourselves how clear it is that Joel's "decision" is one of impulse, and that he has not fully thought through the consequences of his choice. The crucial point is that one's network of beliefs is not only interior; it has a social existence as well. In choosing to delete some portion of that network, one faces the difficulty not only of isolating a fragment of a network that, by its very nature, cannot be divided up into discrete, isolable fragments but of isolating *oneself*, as an agent with beliefs, from other agents whose willful complicity will be required if one's chosen illusion is to have any chance of being maintained.

This is disturbing not only for prudential but, more fundamentally, for moral reasons. To deliberately forget what one has done, after all, is a way of refusing to take responsibility for it. And to the extent that one's existence is located in the shared public realm, to be erased from perception—to be rendered invisible—is quite literally to be done away with; there is an undeniable hostility implicit in the act.

In Milan Kundera's novel *The Book of Laughter and Forgetting*, we find the story of Mirek, a man who, like Joel and Clementine, has had a lover whom he now regrets. In Mirek's case, the affair has been over for more than twenty years; yet he cannot escape his shame at having loved this woman, Zdena, whom he now regards as deeply inappropriate for him. Hoping to destroy the evidence of their relationship, he visits Zdena and asks to borrow the love letters he wrote to her. Sensing, perhaps, that he has no intention of ever returning them, she refuses.

What is perhaps most sinister about Mirek's desire to expunge the memory of a former lover for the sake of his own comfort and convenience, to create an artificial version of reality and thrust it upon others advertised as "the truth," is the way in which this initially self-concerned desire (concerned with one's own sanity, happiness, and mental hygiene) modulates so easily into a desire utterly to deny the reality of the other—the sort of desire that can be found at the heart of the political programs of our most authoritarian regimes. Indeed, *The Book of Laughter and Forgetting* makes explicit the comparison with authoritarianism:

> The reason he wanted to remove her picture from the album of his life was not that he hadn't loved her, but that he had. By erasing her from his mind, he erased his love for her. He airbrushed her out of the picture in the same way the Party propaganda system airbrushed Clementis from the balcony where Gottwald gave his historic speech. Mirek is as much a rewriter of history as the Communist party, all political parties, all nations, all men. People are always shouting they want to create a better future. It's not true. The future is an apathetic

void of no interest to anyone. The past is full of life, eager to irritate us, provoke and insult us, tempt us to destroy or repaint it. The only reason people want to be masters of the future is to change the past. They are fighting for access to the laboratories where photographs are retouched and biographies and histories rewritten.[20]

This passage evokes, even as it inverts, a famous passage from George Orwell's 1984: "Whoever controls the past controls the future. Whoever controls the present controls the past." Of course, one might hope that the amount of evidence one would need to manipulate, and to eliminate, would prove so vast and ungovernable that all such attempts at control through falsification would be doomed to failure. But this only takes us back to the troubling possibility raised by Lydia Davis's story, that the effect of absence of reliable memory, whether individual or communal, will be the undermining of our responsiveness and responsibility to the truth, to the facts, to reality, leaving us in an inherently unstable epistemological predicament in which truth and falsehood become indistinguishable. Hannah Arendt's comments, in the essay she called "Truth and Politics," remind us that the objections to the intentional alteration or erasure of memory are both prudential and moral: we risk doing damage to our communities, our integrity, and our very selves in attempting to alter our pictures of the past:

> [T]he relatively closed systems of totalitarian governments and one-party dictatorships [. . .] are, of course, by far the most effective agencies in shielding ideologies and images from the impact of reality and truth. [. . .] Their trouble is that they must constantly change the falsehoods they offer as a substitute for the real story; changing circumstances require the substitution of one history book for another, the replacement of pages in the encyclopedias and reference books, the disappearance of certain names in favor of others unknown or little known before. And though this continuing instability gives no indication of what the truth might be, it is itself an indication, and a powerful one, of the lying character of all public utterances concerning the factual world . . . [T]he result of a consistent and total substitution of lies for factual truth is not that the lies will now be accepted as truth, and the truth be defamed as lies, but that the sense by which we take our bearings in the real

world—and the category of truth vs falsehood is among the mental means to this end—is being destroyed.[21]

"Replacing history by myth," writes Pierre Vidal-Naquet in a book about Holocaust deniers, "is a procedure that would hardly be dangerous if there were an absolute criterion allowing one to distinguish at first sight between the two." The problem, of course, is that there is no such *absolute* criterion; and, indeed, the effect of the replacement of history with myth is to undermine what progress toward a *pragmatic* distinction we have made. And, as Vidal-Naquet goes on to write, "It is the distinguishing feature of a lie to want to pass itself off as the truth."[22]

"All things are entangled, ensnared, enamored": Affirmation's holism

How could I fail to be grateful to my whole life?

Friedrich Nietzsche[23]

Mirek's motivation, in *The Book of Laughter and Forgetting*, is to deny that he ever loved this woman whom he does not now love. The thought that he might have been wrong, or that he might simply have changed in his likes and tastes, is intolerable to him; in particular, he cannot stand to admit that he had ever loved a woman he now considers ugly, that he could have loved something he now abhors. He is moved by what Ralph Waldo Emerson described as "a reverence for our past act or word, [which we feel] because the eyes of others have no other data for computing our orbit than our past acts, and we are loath to disappoint them."[24] What is unusual about Mirek is only that rather than taking the more common path of trying to make the present fit the past, Mirek's strategy is to alter the past in order to fit the present (as he perceives or imagines it). He wants his life to have the appearance of consistency, coherence, a straight line rather than a crooked path. And he has no faith in Emerson's claim that:

The voyage of the best ship is a zigzag line of a hundred tacks. [. . .] See the line from a sufficient distance, and it straightens itself to the average tendency. Your genuine action will explain itself and will explain your other genuine actions.[25]

Rather, Mirek wants to erase the actual actions and feelings of his past and artificially impose an order upon the history of his loves—as if the various individual moments and movements of his being would only add up to a life worth living if they could all be shown to be pointing in the same direction and to fit snugly against one another like the pieces of a jigsaw puzzle.

Mirek's desire is related to a pair of ideas about love and its relation to life, one true, the other popular but false. The first, true idea is that what one loves reflects, and expresses, the person one is. The second, false idea is that one can only truly love a single person in the course of one's life. This idea exerts a pressure on romantics of a certain sort to deny the reality of past loves, in order to assert a singularity and unity of character over time. It should be admitted that the phenomenology of love itself pushes us, to at least some degree, in this direction: when one is truly in love one's consciousness is taken up quite entirely with the beloved, and it becomes both difficult and to some degree unpleasant to take past feelings and attachments seriously, or remember how vivid and compelling they were to us at the time. Love itself pushes us, in the midst of our experience of it, to romanticize its own nature. Nonetheless it is simply a denial of reality to think that the human person, or the world in which the person lives, is so set up as to guarantee and permit only a single genuine love attachment for each person in the course of a life.

It is hard to avoid the suspicion that Joel's decision to erase Clementine, and hers to delete him, is in part an expression of this desire for consistency, this urge to deny the reality of a past passion that might threaten one's future claims to truly love someone else. Indeed, we might well say of Joel what Kundera says of Mirek, that "The reason he wanted to remove her picture from the album of his life was not that he hadn't loved her, but that he had. By erasing her from his mind, he erased his love for her." When people speak of "moving on" after the end of a relationship, they often mean something very much like this: that the reality of one's previous passion must be downplayed, minimized, even altogether denied so that one may clear one's slate in order to make room for a new and *genuine* passion for someone else who is yet to come along.

But Joel's attempt to follow through in his decision is very nearly derailed. For in the midst of the procedure, Joel comes across a memory of Clementine whose sheer beauty and poignancy strike him afresh. In this memory, in which Joel and Clementine appear to be in bed under the covers, Clementine begins by asking Joel if she is ugly; she then tells the story of an old toy:

> . . . this ugly girl doll who I called Clementine. And I keep yelling at her, "You can't be ugly! Be pretty!" It's weird, like if I could transform her, I would magically change too . . .

Like his other memories of Clementine, this one (which ends with Joel reassuring Clementine that she is indeed pretty, and with an atypically vulnerable Clementine tearfully pleading, "Don't ever leave me. . .") is connected with pain. Yet this does not prevent Joel from recognizing its value and wanting to keep it. Realizing that this memory too will be deleted along with all the others, Joel begins to protest, to yell at Lacuna's team of memory-erasers from within his own mind as if he could be heard. Of course, it may be that he is confused: perhaps he does not realize, or has forgotten, that he cannot keep one memory while discarding the rest. Indeed, this seems to be precisely what he asks for: "Just let me keep this one." But this desire, of course, cannot be satisfied: memories are so intricately and pervasively interrelated that one cannot isolate a single one and preserve it while jettisoning the rest. Indeed, one must wonder how much of its meaning and beauty a single memory that has been wrenched from its context and now exists in absolute isolation could manage to embody. Would such a memory not persist simply as a puzzling and quite possibly disturbing fragment, disconnected from all that might help to make sense of it? At best, perhaps (and perhaps this is what Joel hopes for) it would appear as a scene that one had not in fact experienced in waking life but had imagined or dreamed. But would this really capture the value that the memory, ensconced in its context, bears for Joel? Just how much genuine emotional resonance could a mere dream fragment bear?

If the individual moments in our lives are meaningful and valuable to us precisely because of their connections with other moments in our lives, then the thought that one could hang on to a single beautiful moment while jettisoning the painful context that surrounds it is deeply misguided. Indeed, reflection on the impossibility of this state of affairs may lead us to a view of human life something like one that Nietzsche from time to time expressed:

Have you ever said Yes to a single joy? O my friends, then you have said Yes too to all woe. All things are entangled, ensnared, enamored; if ever you wanted one thing twice, if ever you said "You please me happiness! Abide, moment!" then you wanted all back. All anew, all eternally, all entangled, ensnared, enamored . . . [26]

On Nietzsche's conception, the links between various events (and thus, between various memories) are not only conceptual but *causal*. His view of the deterministic nature of the universe involved the assertion that each particular moment causally implies all others: given a particular event E, and the history H that preceded and led to E, he would assert that *only* H could have led to E; thus, in valuing E we are forced to place a value on H as well:

If we affirm one single moment, we thus affirm not only ourselves but all existence. For nothing is self-sufficient, neither in us ourselves nor in things; and if our soul has trembled with happiness and sounded like a harpstring just once, all eternity was needed to produce this one event—and in this single moment of affirmation all eternity was called good, redeemed, justified, and affirmed.[27]

This gives us, then, our third Nietzschean affirmation thesis:

The Third Affirmation Thesis: There are certain moments in a life that ought to be wholeheartedly affirmed. But to do this, it is necessary to affirm everything in one's life.

For our purposes we can put aside the various worries that quite naturally arise regarding the strong determinism that may seem to underlie this thought. Nietzsche's view, admittedly, involves a metaphysical conception not all will share. But this need not trouble us, for all that is really needed to motivate a version of the Third Affirmation Thesis is the idea that the meaning of a moment depends on its context in one's life— that the lovely moment Joel remembers experiencing with Clementine, for example, is not something that could have occurred between two strangers who lacked the particular shared history that unites these two individuals. We need not, that is, hold that the valued event is *causally* dependent on its history, in a way that implies a single possible course of history; it is enough to hold that the event's *meaning* is not entirely independent of its historical context. This standpoint avoids the controversial metaphysical aspects of Nietzsche's view while still allowing us to endorse the core Nietzschean point that the true affirmer will not be the person who affirms *selectively*, endorsing some moments of her life while wishing others were different, but rather the person who affirms her life as an *entirety*.

Joel's first impulse, then—to save the memory in question, and only this particular memory—shows him to have an understanding of affirmation that is, according to the Third Affirmation Thesis, flawed. But he soon enough comes to realize that what is really at stake is not just the existence of a particular isolated and, as it happens, especially beautiful memory, but the entire existence, for him, of the person that is Clementine, a person who has been the object of his passionate love. And it is at this point that Joel begins to attempt to undermine and outwit the procedure. His goal, then, which begins as the preservation of one particularly lovely and valuable memory of Clementine, soon becomes that of saving *any* memory of Clementine, so that she is not entirely lost to him. Indeed, the strategy he soon hits upon is that of inserting Clementine into a memory in which she does not properly belong—the sort of place where the Lacuna team is least likely to look for her.

In accepting the value of his memories of Clementine, and attempting to save them, Joel is rejecting the romantic view of Mirek: he is pledging himself to acknowledge and take responsibility for an episode in his life that may, from the perspective of his overall life, be considered aberrant, awkward, and in many respects regrettable. Unlike Mirek, who cannot bring himself to admit that he has loved a person who was, by his current standards, imperfect, Joel's recognition that the relationship contained at least one moment of genuine beauty compels him to refrain from denying its reality. In the end, Joel comes to agree with Nietzsche that one cannot affirm such a moment in and of itself without also affirming, at least to a considerable degree, the painful and imperfect sequence of events that forms its broader context. The effect of the Third Affirmation Thesis, at least in such cases, seems to be to discourage us from being the sort of disappointed idealist that condemns the entire world for failing to live up to our utopian standards, and to remind us that a human life can contain moments that are capable of justifying a considerable degree of imperfection.

"A tremendous moment": Affirmation and eternal recurrence

> The renunciation of past and future is the first of all renunciations.
> Simone Weil[28]

Does this mean that Joel must deny having *any* negative feeling or regret regarding Clementine? Nietzsche, it at least sometimes appears, would suggest so:

> My formula for greatness in a human being is *amor fati*: that one wants nothing to be different, not forward, not backward, not in all eternity. Not merely bear what is necessary, still less conceal it—all idealism is mendaciousness in the face of what is necessary—but *love* it.[29]

But does Joel really need to commit himself to a view that is quite this extreme? As I have suggested, many people will probably reject the rigid determinism that, for Nietzsche, underlies the Third Affirmation Thesis. And insofar as the matter is taken to concern not a metaphysical claim about determinism but rather the question of the attitudes we ought to take toward our lives, the essential question, surely, is not whether our attitudes must be *uniformly positive*; it is, rather, whether our attitudes over time must all be *consistent with one another*. In other words, what matters is whether the knowledge of how something began, or of how it will turn out, must necessarily determine our evaluation of that thing in the present moment. If our attitudes must be consistent then affirmation will in many cases be impossible. Facts about the shameful histories that cleared the way for present triumph, for instance, may poison the achievement, thus making it impossible to wholeheartedly endorse it:

> "It was"—that is the name of the will's gnashing of teeth and most secret melancholy. Powerless against what has been done, he is an angry spectator of all that is past. The will cannot will backwards; and that he cannot break time and time's covetousness, that is the will's loneliest melancholy.[30]

Moreover, events in the present will be just as open to being poisoned, sullied, or otherwise undermined by events that lie in the future.

The knowledge that our lives end with the annihilation of death would make it impossible, it might be claimed, for us to affirm their value in the present. Indeed, this claim has been put forward by such Christian thinkers as William Lane Craig with some enthusiasm:

> If each individual person passes out of existence when he dies, then what ultimate meaning can be given to his life? Does it really matter whether he ever existed at all? [. . .] Mankind is a doomed race in a dying universe. Because the human race will eventually cease to exist, it makes no ultimate difference whether it ever did exist. Mankind is thus no more significant than a swarm of mosquitoes or a barnyard of pigs, for their end is all the same. [. . .] Because our lives are ultimately meaningless, the activities we fill our lives with are also meaningless. The long hours spent in study at the university, our jobs, our interests, our friendships—all these are, in the final analysis, utterly meaningless. This is the horror of modern man: because he ends in nothing, he is nothing.[31]

Much of the opposition and downright hostility that Nietzsche felt toward religion, and, in particular, Christianity, can be traced to just this thought. It was the idea that our current life should be devalued with respect to a future life in a different realm—so that the present can have value only if such a future is promised, and, in light of such a promise, the present ought to be sacrificed for the sake of that future—that Nietzsche found not only misguided but offensive. Why, Nietzsche would ask Craig, would the fact of what will happen *later* erase the value of what is happening *now*? Indeed, why think that later facts even *influence* the value of the present? The "future" orientation that is such a deep element of the Christian religion features in many Christian-influenced secular contexts as well—for instance, in utilitarianism and other consequentialist moralities that emphasize the *effects* of one's choice over the nature of the present action in and of itself:

> The most general formula on which every religion and morality is founded is: "Do this and that, refrain from this and that—then you will be happy! Otherwise . . ." Every morality, every religion, is this imperative; I call it the great original sin of reason, the *immortal unreason*. In my mouth, this formula is changed into its opposite—first

example of my "revaluation of all values": a well-turned-out human being, a "happy one," must perform certain actions and shrinks instinctively from other actions; he carries the order, which he represents physiologically, into his relations with other human beings and things. In a formula: his virtue is the *effect* of his happiness.[32]

This gives us our fourth and final Nietzschean thesis regarding affirmation:

> The Fourth Affirmation Thesis: Affirming the value of one's life is a matter of affirming (enough of) the particulars that make up one's life. To affirm a particular one need not deny all that seems inconsistent with it, nor need one affirm everything that is connected with it. One need affirm only the particular *in the present* while giving up the demand for consistency *over time*. One must accept that something that has shameful or evil roots, or that will end in annihilation, failure, or pain, can nevertheless be fully and wholeheartedly endorsed as good *in the present moment*.

I said at the outset of the paper that *Eternal Sunshine of the Spotless Mind* can be viewed as the story of two people who learn to be "immoralists" in the Nietzschean sense. It is now possible to say a bit more concretely just what this means. The Nietzschean affirmer is an "immoralist," in part, because she affirms the value of the present moment without thinking about its future consequences; she wholeheartedly embraces present triumphs and pleasures without evaluating them against a broader framework that would ask such questions as: What will this lead to? What is the ultimate significance of this act for one's own life, for the broader community, or for the history of humanity? If a utopian is one who sees the present moment merely as a means to a more perfect future, then Nietzsche's thought, insofar as it rejects the validity of such future-oriented evaluative perspectives, is in this respect deeply anti-utopian. In his view, the overcoming of *ressentiment* is largely dependent on our learning to be affirmers of this sort; for so long as we insist on imposing a broader, more comprehensive framework of evaluation on our individual actions (rather than viewing them as spontaneous expressions of our characters) we will be unable to avoid clinging to our unacceptable and regrettable pasts, and desiring to take revenge against them. Nor will we be able to free ourselves from the fear and despair that are naturally engendered by the knowledge that, ultimately, all of our cares, plans and goals are doomed to oblivion.

The demands of such a view of affirmation are difficult to meet. Throughout the film Joel and Clementine must frequently remind each other of the importance of valuing the present moment, and of refusing to allow past-directed regrets or future-directed fears to undermine this valuing; just as they must constantly remind each other that integrity, on such a conception, demands the honest acknowledgment of present thoughts and feelings, and the refusal to deny or reject those parts of oneself—one's thoughts, one's loves, one's momentary urges and attractions—that seem not to fit without friction into the sort of artificially smooth and coherent self-describing narrative we are constantly tempted to construct and project for ourselves. The shooting script of *Eternal Sunshine* contains a scene in which Clementine says the following of herself:

> My goal, Joel, is to just let it flow through me? Do you know what I mean? It's like, there's all these emotions and ideas and they come quick and they change and they leave and they come back in a different form and I think we're all taught we should be consistent. Y'know? You love someone—that's it. Forever. You choose to do something with your life—that's it, that's what you do. It's a sign of maturity to stick with that and see things through. And my feeling is that's how you die, because you stop listening to what is true, and what is true is constantly changing.[33]

This is Clementine at her most Emersonian (and, on the reading I am now suggesting, her most Nietzschean). We might compare the famous passage from Emerson's "Self-Reliance":

> But why should you keep your head over your shoulder? Why drag about this monstrous corpse of your memory, lest you contradict somewhat you have stated in this or that public place? Suppose you should contradict yourself; what then? It seems to be a rule of wisdom never to rely on your memory alone, scarcely even in acts of pure memory, but to bring the past for judgment into the thousand-eyed present, and live ever in a new day [. . .] A foolish consistency is the

hobgoblin of little minds, adored by little statesmen and philosophers and divines. With consistency a great soul has simply nothing to do. He may as well concern himself with his shadow on the wall. Speak what you think to-day in words as hard as cannon-balls, and to-morrow speak what to-morrow thinks in hard words again, though it contradict every thing you said to-day.[34]

There is indeed something Emersonian in Clementine's character, in particular, a resistance to planning her actions in advance and to worrying about the consequences that will follow from them. She is described both by herself and by others as "impulsive" (to which Joel replies "It's what I love about you"); she tells Joel "I can't tell from one moment to the next what I'm going to like"; and she (or rather, Joel's interior projection of her) interrupts Joel's fretting about how to prevent his memories from being erased to say "Sweetie, calm down. Enjoy the scenery!" She is also quick to point out Joel's frequent failures to live in the moment, such as his inability to keep from worrying about getting caught when breaking into the house on the beach, or about falling through the ice on the frozen-over Charles River.

Some of her other actions, however, will cause viewers to wonder how deep Clementine's Emersonianism really goes. Most significantly, her impulsive decision to have Joel erased seems less an indication of genuine free-spiritedness than the result of her desire to escape pain and gain revenge; it would seem to be evidence that she is *not* free-spirited but is (rather like Mirek) trapped by the past, dominated by resentment, unable to let things go. (Similarly, her frequent decisions to change her hair color seem to indicate a conscious and artificial desire to *appear* free and spontaneous. As she herself admits—admittedly with an admirable degree of self-awareness—"I apply my personality in a paste.") And in the moments just before the completion of Joel's process of memory annihilation, it is he who must comfort Clementine by reminding her that, while they have only a little time left, there is all the difference in the world between a little time and no time:

CLEMENTINE: This is it, Joel. It's gonna be gone soon.
JOEL: I know.
CLEMENTINE: What do we do?
JOEL: Enjoy it.[35]

Like many moments in *Eternal Sunshine*, this one is, in its way, repeated. At the film's climax, Clementine, shattered by the revelation that she and Joel have already been lovers (and worse, that they have already fallen out of love), attempts to abandon him and flees into the hall. Her decision is highly rational: having heard recordings of themselves describing their reasons for disliking, indeed, *detesting* each other, it has become perfectly clear that any attempt at a romantic relationship is almost certainly doomed to failure. Any relationship that is attempted would now have to take place not only in the light of the devastating comments he has made about her character but also—and this might well be even harder for her to bear— in the light of the deeply cruel things *she* has said about *him*.

Joel, of course, is in the same situation. Yet he follows Clementine out into the hall and calls to her to wait:

> CLEMENTINE: What, Joel? What do you want?
> JOEL: I don't know. (*Pause.*) Just wait. Just wait for a while.
> CLEMENTINE: Okay.
> JOEL: Really?
> CLEMENTINE: I'm not a concept, Joel. I'm just a fucked-up girl who is looking for my own peace of mind. I'm not perfect.
> JOEL: I can't think of anything I don't like about you right now.
> CLEMENTINE: But you will. You will think of things. And I'll get bored with you and feel trapped because that's what happens with me.
> JOEL: Okay.
> (*Pause.*)
> CLEMENTINE: Okay.

These final "okays," which are the last words spoken in the film, are hesitant, uncertain, and somewhat tremulous—but in light of all that faces the lovers they strike a courageous, even thrilling note of affirmation and endorsement. Indeed, the entire episode may well be viewed as a re-enactment of one of Nietzsche's most famous thought experiments, what he called the "eternal recurrence":

> What, if some day or night a demon were to steal after you into your loneliest loneliness and say to you: "This life as you now live it and have lived it, you will have to live once more and innumerable times more; and there will be nothing new in it, but every pain and

every joy and every thought and sigh and everything unutterably small or great in your life will have to return to you, all in the same succession and sequence—even this spider and this moonlight between the trees, and even this moment and I myself. The eternal hourglass of existence is turned upside down again and again, and you with it, speck of dust!"

Would you not throw yourself down and gnash your teeth and curse the demon who spoke thus? Or have you once experienced a tremendous moment when you would have answered him: "You are a god and never have I heard anything more divine." If this thought gained possession of you, it would change you as you are or perhaps crush you. The question in each and every thing, "Do you desire this once more and innumerable times more?" would lie upon your actions as the greatest weight. Or how well disposed would you have to become to yourself and to life to crave nothing more fervently than this ultimate confirmation and seal?[36]

As with the determinism connected with the Third Affirmation Thesis, our main concern is not the metaphysics but the attitude toward life that is here expressed. Indeed, in this passage Nietzsche seems not at all interested in the question of whether history really repeats in an infinite cycle. His concern, rather, is what attitude we would be able to take toward existence if it did, and what this attitude tells us about our attitudes about ourselves and the lives we live. The appearance of the demon is presented as a test, and it is only a certain very rare sort of person who could, in light of the shocking news of the eternal recurrence, respond to this news with joy. It is only in the midst of the "tremendous moment" of which Nietzsche speaks that one achieves true affirmation.

But in addition to the challenge, there is also a liberating aspect to the thought of eternal recurrence. The Fourth Affirmation Thesis expresses the idea that properly valuing the present moment is incompatible with living in a manner that is predominantly oriented toward the future— living, for instance, in the Christian manner of sacrificing one's strength and happiness now in the hope of a later reward. The eternal recurrence, with its cyclical view of history, undermines such linear conceptions. If history is an endlessly repeating loop, then we need not sacrifice the present for the sake of the future. On this conception, each moment is its own future. By conceiving time as a repeating cycle rather than an endlessly forward-moving present moment, the distinction between past, present, and future—and any hierarchy of values grounded in that distinction—is annihilated.

Thus the climax of the film—Joel and Clementine standing in the hall, choosing their fate—can be read as a dramatization of just the sort of "tremendous moment" that the truly free spirit will achieve in the face of the demon's challenge. Joel and Clementine's task is to help each other learn to become so well disposed to themselves, and to life, as "to crave nothing more fervently than this ultimate confirmation and seal." Their task, that is, is to confront without illusion the true nature of their relationship—that the initial infatuation that unites the two is doomed to give way to disappointment, resentment, and even hostility—and to find the strength not to despair in the face of these facts.

In this connection it is interesting to recall what Lacuna's head, Howard Mierzwiak, says to Joel as he urges him to opt for the memory erasure procedure. "This is a personal and profound decision to make," he tells Joel, "but might I suggest that you at least consider the potential pitfalls of a psyche forever spinning its wheels."[37] "Forever spinning its wheels" is an image that might itself remind us of the eternal recurrence. Howard's promise is that Joel will be *released* from the nightmare of eternal recurrence—the endless recurrence of the same memories, pains and regrets. Ironically, though, all the procedure actually does is release Joel into a different kind of cycle of recurrence, one in which he will not only figuratively but *literally* relive the agonies (and, alongside them, the ecstasies) of meeting, falling in love with, and suffering alongside Clementine. In order to overcome, and to master, the tragedy of his fate, Joel must extirpate his longing to be released from it and instead find a way to embrace it, wholeheartedly and with full knowledge and acceptance of its darker aspects.

Conclusion: "The Very Mark of Eros"

> If thou must love me, let it be for naught
> Except for love's sake only . . .
> Elizabeth Barrett Browning, *Sonnets from the Portuguese*[38]

It is important to understand that Nietzsche does not mean to entirely deny the validity of the viewpoint of the future. He would not think that the present perspective ought to be objectively privileged over the future any more than the future perspective should be objectively privileged over the past. (It is the latter, in his view, that happens in Christianity, and in the utilitarian and other ethical views that have arisen in Christianity's wake.) Rather, Nietzsche would deny the idea that any perspective ought to be *objectively* privileged at all. There are, he would insist, only subjective perspectives. Since we always live in the present, the perspective of the present is all that ever really matters. Of course, what is now future will at one point be present; and at that point in time we may have to evaluate our actions and plans very differently than we do now. But the fact that such evaluations will someday be valid does not imply that they are *now* valid.

There is a deep connection here, which I can only suggest and do not have the space to explore, with some of Nietzsche's fundamental ideas about the nature of philosophy. The idea that there exists a privileged "objective" perspective naturally encourages the thought that what is desirable in philosophy is a *comprehensive* view: a complete and systematic theory that will explain and accommodate all of the universe's phenomena, and that can be grasped in a single moment of immense insight. Nietzsche, by contrast, was a deeply and pervasively anti-systematic philosopher.[39] He was interested in the integrity of each philosophical insight as it presented itself to him, and was little troubled by the fact that a certain insight, which struck him *now* as a valid and illuminating view into the nature of existence, might not be capable of being reconciled with *other* insights that had also struck him, on various occasions, as valid and illuminating. (His thought was, in this as in many other respects, genuinely Emersonian.) Indeed, this phenomenon is apparent in the four Nietzschean affirmation theses I have identified in this paper. The four do not add up to anything like a system; on the contrary, to a considerable degree they tend to oppose and even undermine one another. Yet each represents, I think, a genuine insight, and thus offers the possibility of a kind of response to the challenge of affirmation.

It is the Fourth Affirmation Thesis that I find the most profound, the most insightful, and also the most troubling. As I have said, it suggests a view of life that is difficult to fully and consistently embody; yet there is, one might insist, a great value in our striving to do so. It may be, too, that love is the human phenomenon that most encourages such strivings.

For love—the love, at any rate, that is connected with passion and eros—demands to be experienced as fully present in the immediate moment; it mocks and rejects past and future claims and commitments that would narrow or impinge on its domain; and indeed, to a certain extent it makes it difficult for us even to perceive such competing claims.

Ironically, the most eloquent statement I know of the link between erotic love and the sort of affirmation we have in mind is found not in Nietzsche but in the writings of the Christian philosopher C. S. Lewis:

> Eros does not aim at happiness. We may think he does, but when he is brought to the test it proves otherwise. Everyone knows that it is useless to try to separate lovers by proving to them that their marriage will be an unhappy one. This is not only because they will disbelieve you. They usually will, no doubt. But even if they believed, they would not be dissuaded. For it is the very mark of Eros that when he is in us we had rather share unhappiness with the Beloved than be happy on any other terms. Even if the two lovers are mature and experienced people who know that broken hearts heal in the end and can clearly foresee that, if they once steeled themselves to go through the present agony of parting, they would almost certainly be happier ten years hence than marriage is at all likely to make them—even then, they would not part. To Eros all these calculations are irrelevant—just as the coolly brutal judgment of Lucretius is irrelevant to Venus. Even when it becomes clear beyond all evasion that marriage with the Beloved cannot lead to happiness—when it cannot even profess to offer any other life than that of tending an incurable invalid, of hopeless poverty, of exile, or of disgrace—Eros never hesitates to say, "Better this than parting. Better to be miserable with her than happy without her. Let our hearts break provided they break together." If the voice within us does not say this, it is not the voice of Eros.[40]

Let our hearts break provided they break together. What better statement of Joel and Clementine's ultimate aspiration could we desire? Indeed, *Eternal Sunshine of the Spotless Mind* is surely one of the most romantic movies ever made. Other movies cheapen love by regarding it as nothing more than the gateway to pleasure and success. Sunnier and more optimistic by nature, but less confident in the value of passion, they insist on justifying love in terms of something other than itself. The happy couple, united (typically in marriage) in the film's finale, revels in the anticipation of the blissful and prosperous future they have been promised. And so one cannot help but wonder: do these two *really* love each other, or are they merely in love with their own anticipated joy? Whereas one cannot doubt that Joel and Clementine are true lovers. Knowing how badly things will turn out—that they will live not happily, but miserably, ever after—they nonetheless pledge themselves to each other. It is, indeed, "the very mark of Eros" whose stamp we are witnessing.

In the film's final exchange, behind Clementine's voice, speaking its single, hesitant yet celebratory "Okay," there seems to me to be a second, very nearly audible voice. That voice is also Clementine's: perhaps we would hear it if the film chose to take us into the largely unknown territory of *her* head. And that we cannot hear it does not matter, for we can see it in Clementine's face, in the ecstatic and finally comprehending smile that breaks across her features as Joel responds with his own calm and accepting "Okay" to the litany of sufferings and despairs that are in store for them. *You are a god,* this voice tells Joel. *And never have I heard anything more divine.*[41]

Notes

1 Friedrich Nietzsche, *On the Genealogy of Morals*, trans. Walter Kaufmann, in Nietzsche 1992, p. 475 (first essay, section 10).
2 Pinsky 1999, pp. 60–70; p. 70.
3 Austen 1991, p. 21.
4 Nietzsche, *Beyond Good and Evil*, section 70, in Nietzsche 1992, p. 270.
5 Santayana 1924, p. 284.
6 Nietzsche, *Beyond Good and Evil*, section 217. The Kaufmann translation (Nietzsche 1992, p. 336) reads differently: "Blessed are the forgetful: for they get over their stupidities, too."
7 Nietzsche, *Twilight of the Idols*, in Nietzsche 1954, p. 491.
8 Austen 1991, p. 376.
9 Nietzsche, *On the Genealogy of Morals*, second essay, section 1, in Nietzsche 1992, p. 493.
10 Nietzsche, *The Will to Power*, section 609, cited in Nehamas 1995, p. 69.
11 Nietzsche 1995, p. 89.
12 Nietzsche, *On the Genealogy of Morals*, in Nietzsche 1992, pp. 493–4 (second essay, section 1).
13 Nietzsche, *Beyond Good and Evil*, section 68, in Nietzsche 1992, p. 270.
14 Kaufman 2004, p. 58.

15 Varlam Shalamov, *Kolyma Tales*, cited in Gray 2003, pp. 100–1.
16 Nietzsche, *Beyond Good and Evil*, section 39, in Nietzsche 1992, p. 239.
17 Philosophical theories making memory the basis of personal identity go back at least to John Locke's *Essay Concerning Human Understanding* (Locke 1975).
18 Davis 1997, p. 136.
19 Frankfurt 2006, pp. 78–9.
20 Kundera 1982, p. 22.
21 Hannah Arendt, "Truth and Politics," in Arendt 1977, pp. 256–7.
22 Vidal-Naquet 1992, pp. 50–1.
23 Nietzsche, from the epigraph to *Ecce Homo*, in Nietzsche 1992, p. 677.
24 Ralph Waldo Emerson, "Self-Reliance," in Emerson 1891, p. 64.
25 Emerson, "Self-Reliance," in Emerson 1891, p. 66.
26 Nietzsche, *Thus Spoke Zarathustra*, in Nietzsche 1954, p. 435.
27 *The Will to Power*, section 1032, quoted in Nehamas 1995, p. 232.
28 Simone Weil, in Westphal and Levinson 1993, p. 221.
29 Nietzsche, *Ecce Homo*, in Nietzsche 1992, p. 714.
30 Nietzsche, *Thus Spake Zarathustra*, second part, in Nietzsche 1954, p. 251.
31 Craig 2000, p. 42.
32 Nietzsche, *Twilight of the Idols*, in Nietzsche 1954, p. 493.
33 Kaufmann 2004, pp. 19–20.
34 Emerson, "Self-Reliance," in Emerson 1891, pp. 64–5.
35 The poignancy of the moment is only increased when we recall that this is the *imagined* Clementine. Joel's time with the *real* Clementine has already run out: she has forgotten him. Moreover, while in the film this exchange ends with Joel saying "Enjoy it," in the shooting script (Kaufman 2004, p. 101) Joel adds two more words: "Say goodbye."
36 Nietzsche, *The Gay Science*, section 341; quoted in Nehamas 2001, p. 125.
37 Kaufman 2004, p. 34.
38 Browning 1992.
39 Though this claim is of course complicated by some of his remarks regarding the "will to power."
40 Lewis, pp. 106–7.
41 Much of this paper was written at the Stanford Humanities Center while I was on sabbatical from California State University, Chico. I am grateful to both institutions for their support.

References

Arendt, Hannah (1977) *Between Past and Future: Eight Exercises in Political Thought*, New York: Penguin.
Austen, Jane (1991) *Pride and Prejudice*, Norwalk, CT: The Easton Press.
Browning, Elizabeth Barrett (1992) *Sonnets from the Portuguese, and Other Poems*, Mineola, NY: Dover Publications.

Craig, William Lane (2000) "The Absurdity of Life Without God," in E. D. Klemke (ed.) *The Meaning of Life*, 2nd edition, New York: Oxford University Press.

Davis, Lydia (1997) *Almost No Memory*, New York: Farrar, Straus, Giroux.

Emerson, Ralph Waldo (1891) *Essays: First Series*, Philadelphia, PA: David McKay.

Frankfurt, Harry (2006) *On Truth*, New York: Knopf.

Gray, John (2003) *Straw Dogs*, London: Granta Books.

Kaufman, Charlie (2004) *Eternal Sunshine of the Spotless Mind: The Shooting Script*, New York: Newmarket Press.

Kundera, Milan (1982) *The Book of Laughter and Forgetting*, Boston, MA: Faber & Faber.

Lewis, C. S. (1960) *The Four Loves*, New York: Harcourt, Brace & Co.

Locke, John (1975) *Essay Concerning Human Understanding*, ed. Peter H. Nidditch, Oxford: Clarendon Press.

Nehamas, Alexander (1995) *Nietzsche: Life as Literature*, Cambridge, MA: Harvard University Press.

_____ (2001) "Eternal Recurrence," in Brian Leiter (ed.) *Nietzsche*, New York: Oxford University Press.

Nietzsche, Friedrich (1954) *The Portable Nietzsche*, New York: The Viking Press.

_____ (1992) *Basic Writings of Nietzsche*, New York: The Modern Library.

_____ (1995) "On the Utility and Liability of History for Life," in *Unfashionable Observations*, trans. Richard T. Gray, Stanford, CA: Stanford University Press.

Pinsky, Robert (1999) "Poetry and American Memory," *Atlantic Monthly*, October 1999.

Santayana, George (1924) *The Life of Reason*, 2nd ed., New York: Scribner.

Vidal-Naquet, Pierre (1992) *Assassins of Memory*, trans. Jeffrey Mehlman, New York: Columbia University Press.

Westphal, Jonathan, and Carl Levinson (eds) (1993) *Time*, Indianapolis, IN: Hackett Publishing Company.

Chapter 4

Valerie Tiberius

BAD MEMORIES, GOOD DECISIONS, AND THE THREE JOELS

MEMORIES DISTORT THE PAST. To take a fitting example, a friend of mine remembered the ending of *Eternal Sunshine* as a rather depressing condemnation of the possibility of love. In her memory, the film ended with Joel and Clementine going their separate ways after discovering that they had once been together and had come to hate each other. In fact, the film ends with Joel and Clementine apparently ready to try again. I showed my friend the end of the film again, and she was stunned by the finale. She then recalled that she was going through a painful break-up herself the first time she watched the film and that this must have colored what she remembered about it.

The phenomenon of memory distortion, of course, is not confined to our memories of films. Psychologists have shown that memory of pain misrepresents the actual experience of pain by weighing the peak and end of the experience more heavily than the duration.[1] In other words, when we retrospectively assess an experience we tend to focus most on what we remember as the best (or worst) part of it and on how it ended in order to formulate a judgment about how good or bad the experience was as a whole. This distorting effect of memory is evident in *Eternal Sunshine*. When Joel wants to have Clementine erased from his memory, he is remembering the worst of their times together, one of which is the end of their time together. We can imagine that Clementine's decision to erase Joel was similarly influenced by their last moments together. Joel's cruel remark that Clementine sleeps with people in order to get them to like her affects her deeply and causes her to storm out of the apartment. Joel doesn't think about the good memories of Clem when he makes the decision to have her erased, and we can imagine that Clem's decision to erase Joel was similarly biased.

If our memories distort the past, what does this mean for our ability to make good decisions? How should we make decisions, given that our memories are what they are? The film suggests several different answers to this question by showing us how Joel changes in response to changes in the information he has. There are (metaphorically speaking) at least three Joels, each of whom would make a decision about Clementine in a different way: the *bitter* Joel, who makes the tape detailing Clementine's faults before erasing her from his memory; the *spotless* Joel, whose memory has been erased and who has just had the experience of spending 24 hours with Clem; and the *sadder but wiser* Joel, whose memory has been erased and who has just listened to the tape that the first Joel made. Which of these Joels would we want to say is in the best position for making a decision about whether to continue his relationship with Clem?

I will argue in this essay that there is much to be said in favor of Sadder-but-wiser Joel from the standpoint of philosophical and common sense conceptions of good decision-making that emphasize the importance of a calm, cool point of view. Now we might think that if a conception of good decision-making makes brain damage look like a good idea, then so much the worse for that conception. But I do not think this is the right conclusion to draw. On the contrary, I think that the distance Joel achieves from his bad memories and their attendant emotional responses allows him to make a better decision than the one Bitter Joel made to have his memory erased. It is a good thing, then, if a conception of good decision-making suggests we should approve of Sadder-but-wiser Joel. Nevertheless, I do think that an exclusive focus on a calm, cool point of view misses the important fact that the distanced point of view is not *always* the right one from which to make decisions. Sadder-but-wiser Joel would be in a bad position to make a decision about Clementine if his circumstances were different.

These reflections on Joel and ideals of good decision-making lead me to defend a more flexible account, according to which the best perspective to have when making decisions or engaging in practical reasoning varies with the circumstances. The account builds in flexibility in another way, too, the need for which is also highlighted by the film. We can learn from Joel that the difficulty in overcoming painful memories may call for desperate measures. To make good decisions, then, we may need to be open to a variety of methods for achieving the right perspective with the right emotional cast. All this flexibility invites questions about the notion of the self that underlies my account of good decision-making and how a person making decisions in the way I recommend can take themselves to be self-directed. These questions will be addressed in the third section of the paper.

The spotless mind and Bitter Joel

Michael Meyer has eloquently argued that Eternal Sunshine of the Spotless Mind demonstrates the importance of memories—both the painful and the pleasant ones—to our ability to make good judgments about the future. The "central story of Eternal Sunshine ingeniously highlights how Joel's forgetting of Clementine has various distinct but related disadvantages that go well beyond his incurring the liability of repeating past mistakes."[2] In addition to handicapping judgment, Meyer argues, forgetting painful events from the past precludes forgiveness and reconciliation between friends.

Surely it is right to say that Joel and Clem, freshly cleansed of their memories of each other, are not in a good position to make decisions.

A person with a spotless mind is, as Mary (Lacuna Inc.'s devoted secretary) puts it, like a baby: "pure, free, clean." But such a person is not wise; a baby has no information and has no lessons from experience. An ending in which Joel and Clem get together after their memories are erased, without coming across the tapes from Lacuna Inc., would be a tragic ending. We would have no reason not to conclude that they are doomed to do things exactly as they did before, making all the same mistakes, learning nothing once again.[3]

Joel of the spotless mind is not wise. Meyer's argument might imply that Bitter Joel, the Joel who decides to go to Lacuna Inc., is a better judge, a wiser person.[4] Is he? I would suggest that when Joel and Clementine are steeped in the painful memories of their break-up, they are also not well situated to exercise good judgment. This is, after all, the position from which they each decide to have their memories wiped clean. Nor are they in a good position to forgive or reconcile; in fact, forgiveness seems to be the furthest thing from their minds. The problem is that Bitter Joel is experiencing memory distortion and the emotional overload that can accompany it. He does not survey all the memories of his relationship with Clem, taking in the good and the bad. Rather, he fixates on his recent discovery that Clem has had him erased and the memory of her at the bookstore kissing another man, failing to recognize Joel at all. These memories cause deep sadness and resentment. Unbalanced by any positive emotions he might have had were he to remember other aspects of their relationship, these feelings lead him to Lacuna Inc.

Our emotional outlook may color the memories that we have, or direct us to remember certain events rather than others. Further, the emotions that are prompted by our selective and often distorted memories do not necessarily represent the whole of our personalities. For example, if we are naturally inclined to put more weight on the end of an experience, and if the end of the experience was emotionally stressful, this could lead us to be more influenced by the negative emotions than we would be if we remembered the experience more fully. If memories and emotions track and influence each other in this way, then it seems that we can be in the grip of a pair of memories and emotions in the same way that we can be overwhelmed by a passion in the heat of the moment.

Now one might think that if we are going to remember, say, the end of an experience more than other aspects of it, then we should be more greatly influenced by the emotions that track that memory. In other words, if Joel is going to remember seeing Clem kissing another man in the bookstore more than he remembers any of the good experiences they had together, then perhaps it will indeed be best for him to be influenced by the emotions that surround the painful memory. After all, that memory will lead him to avoid women like Clem, which will mean fewer painful experiences in the future. On this way of thinking, it is the Joel whose memories have not been touched who makes the best decisions.

This objection makes the dubious assumption that if powerful emotions and painful memories are pervasive and long-lasting parts of our personality, then they will lead us in the direction of our overall, long-term good. Joel's memory of Clem in the bookstore and its attendant jealousy and resentment will lead Joel in the right direction only if it is good for him to indulge these motives and protect himself from any future causes of them. But it's far from clear that this is how things stand. Even if Joel is always going to be a jealous mess, a life in which he never risks incurring feelings of jealousy is unlikely to be the best one for him. Adults are "a mess of sadness and phobias," Mary says when she compares the state that Bitter Joel is in to the state of a baby. Letting that mess determine what we do isn't necessarily the best course.

Mary's decision to erase Howard Mierzwiak from her memory provides another example. We do not see Mary make this decision in the film, but we can guess that it was prompted by a great deal of sadness and dejection, perhaps caused by being (ultimately) rejected by Howard. It seems clear from what happens later that this decision was not best for Mary in the long term, since she falls for Howard a second time and causes herself the same grief all over again. Mary's case is complicated by the fact that it is unclear how much of this decision was really hers; Mrs Mierzwiak suggests that this decision was manipulated by Howard, at least to some degree. Nevertheless, insofar as Mary was susceptible to convincing due to the sadness engendered by a sticky memory of rejection, the decision she made in this state would not seem to be best for her in the long term.

Even if our memory of the end of an experience shapes our assessment of the whole, and even if it will continue to do so, making decisions in the grip of a distorting emotion/memory pair is unlikely to be good for us. To see why in more detail, we need to think about how we can learn from our painful memories and our emotional responses to them in a way that will actually improve our judgment. It's plausible to think that one of the things Joel needs to learn from his relationship with Clementine is that he has a tendency to stifle his feelings until they well up out of control in mean outbursts to the person he loves. It might also be useful for him to learn that he is attracted to impulsive, flamboyant women who provide a contrast to his staid personality, and also that he isn't quite comfortable with the impulsiveness or flamboyance once he has to live with it. Certainly, he won't learn any of these things by forgetting all. But he also won't learn these lessons by dwelling on the memories that are most conspicuous. To learn these lessons, he needs to think about many aspects of his relationship with Clem and many emotional patterns. He shouldn't just think about the worst and last, and he shouldn't just focus on his anger, jealousy, and sadness. Further, he needs to consider his anger, jealousy, and sadness without being overpowered by them.

The point here is the familiar one that it is unwise to make decisions in the heat of the moment (as, for example, when seething with jealousy or rage). This point is part of a venerable conception of good decision-making that recommends a "calm, cool" moment for deliberation.[5] This advice is also part of common sense. ("Wait until you cool down to make that decision.") If you think that the best standpoint from which to make decisions or engage in practical reasoning is the calm and cool one, then you are likely to think that Joel's decision to have his memory erased is unfortunately hot-headed and that Mary's is miserably rash. Of course, Spotless Joel is in a different but also unfortunate position with respect to decision-making. This leads us to consider the possibility that Sadder-but-wiser Joel—who is missing some of the obvious faults of the other two—is actually in the best position to make good decisions.

My favoring Sadder-but-wiser Joel and associating him with a model of good decision-making depends on thinking that the film's ending is a hopeful one. It is worth saying something about why I think the film's ending is hopeful, since this doesn't seem to be a universal interpretation. The pessimistic interpretation of the ending would be that without painful memories we are doomed to repeat the same mistakes over and over again. The final conversation we see between Joel and Clem could lend itself to this interpretation. He tells her he doesn't think all the bad things about her that he says on the tape. She points out that he will, and that she will become bored with him "because that's what I do." He responds, "OK." I think it is overly pessimistic to interpret Joel's response as accepting that they will repeat the same mistakes. Learning that they made the mistakes they made will change how they go forward and Joel must know this. While Joel does seem to be willing to risk repeating the same mistakes, the hope is that they will be able to avoid them. I also think it is overly pessimistic for us as the audience to be certain that Joel and Clem will repeat their mistakes—or, at least, that they will repeat them so exactly that once again neither will recognize the value of what they have been through.

Furthermore, the decision that Joel makes in the hallway to give it another try with Clem seems to me a better decision than his decision to erase her from his memory. This is another way in which the film's ending is hopeful. After all, we have just seen (through Joel's memory) many wonderful moments that Joel and Clem had together. This part of the film is warm and romantic. They are good together: she makes him feel alive, he makes her feel beautiful, and they have chemistry, a fact which is made more striking by the comparison to Clem's relationship with the creepy Patrick.

Sadder-but-wiser Joel and the importance of emotions

Spotless Joel has no experiences to learn from, but Bitter Joel learns the wrong lessons because of the distortion of memory. For this reason, I favor Sadder-but-wiser Joel as the better judge. Sadder-but-wiser Joel is at least not in the grip of anger and jealousy when he makes his decisions. Research in psychology suggests that we have a tendency to remember the worst part of a bad experience more vividly than the rest of the experience, or to put more weight on the worst part in our retrospective assessment of the whole. I have been suggesting that these painful memories give rise to painful emotions that may be inappropriate to the facts of the situation when the worst bit is put into context. Putting these two facts of human experience together, we can see that making judgments on the basis of our emotionally laden memories can sometimes be problematic. Sadder-but-wiser Joel is in a better position because his emotional disengagement from the memories allows him to put them into context.

Even if Sadder-but-wiser Joel is a better decision-maker than his Spotless or Bitter versions, however, one might still balk at thinking of him as the paradigm of a good decision-maker. This is for at least two reasons: First, emotions—even powerful negative emotions—can give us information that is crucial to good judgment, and Sadder-but-wiser

Joel does not feel those emotions. If you think that being in the emotional state is crucial to decision-making, then too much distance can be a problem. Second, even if the emotionally distanced state of mind is the right point of view, one might wonder whether we can really choose to remember our pasts as if by reading about them in a book. In the absence of the futuristic technology in Lacuna Inc., one might think that this advice isn't very practical.

We need to make sure that claiming an advantage in decision-making for Sadder-but-wiser Joel does not conflict with some truths about the importance of emotions. First of all, as psychologists such as Antonio Damasio[6] have shown, rational decision-making requires affect. People who have damage to the part of the brain that stores emotional memory make terrible decisions and become paralyzed by trivial choices, even though they have no other cognitive defects. Of course Sadder-but-wiser Joel is not brain damaged in this way. Joel at the end of the film is experiencing positive emotions toward Clem because of the time they have just spent together. He is also experiencing confusion and sadness after listening to the news about his past with Clem. Nor is Butler's ideal calm, cool deliberator entirely unemotional; rather, he is guided by the calm passions of self-love and benevolence. Joel is missing only the powerful feelings of anger, jealousy, and resentment that seem to cloud and distort the fuller picture of his relationship with Clem.[7]

Given this, the second point about emotions that we should consider is that we do learn valuable things from bad experiences and from powerful, painful emotions such as anger. As feminists have long argued, anger can often tell us when we are not being treated as we deserve to be.[8] Clem and Joel both learn useful things from listening to their own and each other's tapes, and, importantly, they would not have made the tapes in the first place had they not at one point remembered the events that happened in a personal way, and felt all the emotions that those memories produced. Therefore, my suggestion that the Sadder-but-wiser Joel is a better judge does not imply that we should try not to experience anger or other powerful emotions. Sadder-but-wiser Joel does learn from his anger, though he isn't feeling it at the time of the lesson; he is in the unique position of being able to learn something from these powerful emotions without being overpowered by them.

But now we might wonder whether Sadder-but-wiser Joel's unique position is really the best position. After all, it isn't clear that the lessons of painful experiences will have the same effect when learned second hand. We aren't generally very good at learning from others' mistakes. Why would we be any better at learning from our own mistakes if we related to the self who had made those mistakes as a different person? The knowledge we need to make better decisions is practical knowledge that motivates us to change our behavior or way of thinking; just learning some facts about what happened to us in the past may not be a sufficient replacement. Particularly if what we need to learn is what is really important to us, regaining the affective charge of the memories may be crucial.

Another problem with recommending Sadder-but-wiser Joel is that his advantage in decision-making seems to depend on his circumstances. Had things been different, we could imagine the decision of Bitter Joel being correct, or at least preferable to Sadder-but-Wiser Joel's decision to give it another go with Clem. The case in favor of extreme distancing depends on the assumption that our emotions and memory are indeed *distorting* the past. They might not be. In such cases, we may be better off making a decision from within that emotional perspective. To illustrate this point, recall Clementine's response to Joel telling her that she sleeps with people to get them to like her. If Joel's memory is accurate, it is this event that is the catalyst for her to storm out of the apartment and have her memory cleansed. In the film, we can see her reaction as impulsive and out of proportion because we do not think that Joel is a cruel person. He is a confused, jealous, somewhat immature person who lashes out in a mean way because he doesn't know what else to do. Joel's words hit a raw nerve and Clem can't recover from it. Granted, a loving partner *shouldn't* say things that he knows will hit a nerve and be extremely hurtful to his beloved even in the heat of the moment. But Clem is also confused and immature, and she too says hurtful things in the heat of the moment. This kind of failure—unlike being genuinely cruel—is not necessarily grounds for metaphorical or literal erasure. But we can certainly imagine circumstances that would make abandoning Joel more appropriate. Sometimes a person can say or do something to you that is unforgivable precisely because it reveals something about that person's true character. If we thought that Joel's expression was evidence that he is a cruel person, Clem's reaction would have been more understandable. If Joel was an abusive, domineering nightmare of a person, we would be glad about Clem's decision to get him out of her life.[9]

Mary provides another example of someone who makes what seems to be a good decision in a hot-headed state. When she learns from Howard's wife that she has had a crush on Howard before, and that her memories of this were erased, she is very upset. She storms off, we imagine, in a fit of anger, disappointment, and confusion. In this state, she makes a decision to expose what Dr Mierzwiak has been doing to his patients. This decision is one she would never have made before she discovered the truth about herself; it may also be one that she couldn't have made (or followed through on) without the motivational boost from her anger.

So, sometimes it is good to be in a calm, cool, deliberative moment when one makes decisions, but sometimes one is better off being in a powerful emotional state. The emotional perspective from which one is best situated to make decisions, in my view, can vary with the circumstances. One might object to this picture because one thinks that we can always make decisions that are indicated by powerful emotions such as anger without actually being in those emotions at the time. For example, a person could learn from their anger that they must leave their abusive partner, but then make the decision to leave after the anger has subsided. I do not deny that this sometimes happens, but it's not clear that it's always possible.[10] Notice that it is not necessary to advocate making decisions in full heated rage in order to advocate moving away from the view that the calm, cool point of view is always the right one. We experience emotions in degrees and we can experience different emotions simultaneously; the best point of view from which to decide to leave an abuser, or to right another kind of injustice, might be one that is infused with anger, though not exclusively and not to its most extreme degree.

The point that the best state of mind for making decisions varies with context might be made more intuitive if we think about positive emotions. There are some decisions we make out of love or joy that we probably would not make if we were in a calmer, cooler emotional state. Certain acts of courage and generosity seem to be like this. Or take, for example, a person who visits a factory farm in order to engage his sympathy and compassion in such a way that he is able to commit himself to vegetarianism. Such commitments don't always last, but the point is that it is plausible to think that the decision made when the person is at their most sympathetic and compassionate is the better decision. Again, the case for the calm, cool perspective is based on the assumption that the violent, hot emotions distort the facts. In the case of the aspiring vegetarian, the powerful positive emotions are not distorting. (For those who find this example unpersuasive, we can think of others. For instance, one might force oneself to read the biographies of malnourished children on the Oxfam website in order to get oneself to donate more money to the cause.)

The picture of good decision-making we have arrived at is complicated. There is no one emotional state of mind that is best for making all decisions; rather, we are better off having distance from distorting emotions and the memories that accompany them, but emotions that are not distorting may be necessary for good decisions. Further, when we are overwhelmed by emotional memories that distort the past, we need ways of regaining perspective. A good decision-maker, then, needs to be able to navigate these different emotional states of mind, and this raises some practical questions.

First, if it is sometimes best to experience painful memories, learn their lessons, and then put ourselves emotionally out of their reach, a question arises about how to take this advice. How can we create the kind of distance that Joel (and Clementine) have from their painful, emotionally infused memories at the end of the film? Taken as a very practical question about what kinds of techniques will work for us, this is really a subject for psychologists and not one about which philosophers have any particular expertise. For example, Daniel Goleman suggests that married couples who fight should take their pulse during arguments and put themselves in a 20 minute time-out when their pulse rate goes above a certain level.[11] Philosophers are not in a position to give this kind of advice. We can, however, point to the kind of advice that is appropriate. If psychologists are correct that certain emotions (such as anger) change our physiology in lasting ways, we need strategies that allow us to pause (for at least 20 minutes, according to Goleman) before making a decision in anger. Further, given what we know from experience about how difficult it can be to achieve distance from emotions we regard as inappropriate, strategies that do not just rely on efforts of will would also be helpful. One lesson we might learn from Joel's experience is that the ability to regard part of yourself from the third person point of view is a helpful trick. Strategies that produce this effect in a non-literal way would be welcome.

Second, if we are sometimes in the situation discussed above (in need of emotional distance) and sometimes not, how do we decide which position we're in? How do we know whether we're the victim of a distorting emotional memory or finally seeing things clearly? There might be some clues to emotional distortion. If you find when you review the past that your thoughts are stuck on one or two incidents, and that you aren't thinking much at all about the larger context, this might be evidence that you are following the "peak/end" rule, which would be evidence of distortion. In general, though, it's not easy to know whether your thinking is distorted or not from the inside, and sometimes it might be downright impossible. This is not an objection to my conception of good decision-making; it's just the point that sometimes we aren't going to be able to make good decisions.

Erasure, distance, and self-direction

According to the picture of good decision-making I've described so far we need to be able to adopt different emotional perspectives for decision-making depending on the circumstances, and we need to be able both to learn from and to distance ourselves from painful, distorting memories. This picture seems to assume a somewhat divided, disunified self— we have different emotional guises that lead us to make decisions in different ways and we need to find ways of coping with these multiple facets of ourselves. This raises a problem for the picture I have drawn so far, namely, the problem of how to reconcile the idea that there isn't a single best perspective from which to make decisions with the ideal of self-direction.

Before explaining further what the problem is here, it will help to elaborate on the cause. As I have been picturing good judgment, we sometimes need to learn from painful memories that have the power to overwhelm us. The picture I have drawn is not one according to which we fully integrate the various facets of our personality to distill a single lesson. Rather, I have suggested that we need to keep these facts in mind but also try to achieve some critical distance from them. When we use the usual methods for trying to distance ourselves from painful memories (waiting, meditating, and so on), unlike Joel, we remember being the person who was in the grip of the worst of an experience. Further, in real life (without Lacuna Inc.), the process by which we achieve distance from painful memories can be lengthy and circuitous. During this process, painful memories and emotions can come back and possess us again, making it unclear from the first person point of view which is the voice with authority.

If I am right that painful memories are both sources of knowledge that improve judgment and sources of distortion that impede good judgment, then the process discussed above may be important and, practically speaking, inevitable. In the effort to make good judgments, we may just be stuck with multiple perspectives that ebb and flow. The problem here is that acknowledging multiple perspectives can have the effect of making us think we are of two (or more) minds, and this divided self-image could disturb the sense in which we take ourselves to be in control, the director of our own lives. Achieving distance from painful memories in such a way that we can learn the right lessons from them creates more than one voice in our heads and it may not be clear from the inside who is really in charge. The fact that we are sometimes better off deciding from an emotionally charged state of mind makes things even worse. Our emotional outlooks change, and which outlook we have will affect the choices we make.

If I am right that there is no single emotional outlook that is the right one for all decisions, then there seems to be a sense in which there are different possible directors. The problem this raises is the problem of how to maintain a sense of ourselves as self-directed, while at the same time recognizing that we have different parts that cannot all be in full force at the same time, more than one of which is sometimes best suited to be in charge of making decisions. One might think that this way of putting the problem assumes an overly demanding notion of a unified self. This may be so, but I would maintain that this notion—according to which there is one perspective, one rational point of view, from which to make choices—is a notion of unity that philosophers have found attractive. Of course, philosophers don't agree on what this perspective is. Some, such as Bishop Butler, think of it in terms of particular passions such as self-love and benevolence, while Kantians think that the right perspective is defined in terms of respect and rational principles.

Some readers may think that the obvious answer is that we cannot continue to think of ourselves as self-directed and that this is not anything to be worried about. I think the tolerant spirit of this answer is on the right track, but I do not want to give up on self-direction as part of our self-conception and an ideal to strive for. Instead, I suggest that we change our vision of just what self-direction requires. In particular, we ought to understand self-direction in a way that does not require a single perspective from which to make decisions, unified by a specific set of passions or principles.

Some philosophers think that to be self-directed, or autonomous, we must be coherent, unified agents. For example, Christine Korsgaard, a staunch defender of this view, argues that:

> it is essential to the concept of agency that an agent be unified. That is to say: to regard some movement of my mind or my body as my action, I must see it as an expression of my self as a whole, rather than as a product of some force that is at work on me or in me. Movements that result from forces working on me or in me constitute things that happen to me.[12]

According to Korsgaard, to see yourself as an agent at all, you must see yourself as the single author of your actions. Because the process of learning from painful memories while trying to put them in perspective is a process during which we are not really unified agents, on this view we cannot really see ourselves as self-directed agents while engaged in this process. The thought here is that this process includes emotional outlooks that are not expressions of oneself "as a whole" and are indeed partly the product of outside forces. I am suggesting that we should nevertheless regard these emotional stages as parts of ourselves and, moreover, that it makes sense at some times but not others for them to be at play in our decision-making.

Given how frequently we are "of two minds," the importance of learning from parts of ourselves that should not have full authority, and the important but intermittent role that intense emotions can have in decision-making, I think Korsgaard's requirement on agency is too restrictive. Moreover, sometimes it is very unclear which parts of ourselves we should identify with and which we should try to gain distance from. To say that as long as it remains unclear we are not really agents directing our own lives is to rule out a lot of important activity from the domain of self-direction. To illustrate the point, imagine Joel in the hallway at the end of the film, but imagine that instead of having his memory erased he has taken steps to put these memories in perspective—to remember the good as well as the bad, to distance himself from the powerful emotions that attach to the worst memory of Clementine. Imagine too, as seems likely, that Joel is still not entirely sure that his anger wasn't appropriate, though he's willing now to entertain this possibility seriously. According to the conception of agency that demands unity, Joel's agency is impugned by the fact that he is *coping* with competing forces, living with them rather than trying to eliminate all the contradictions. Alternatively, according to the conception of agency I am advocating, coping with competing forces is one of the things we do as agents; Joel can be self-directed by "trying on" an aspect of himself as the one with which to identify in the context without thereby committing himself to treating the competing aspect of self as an alien force.

(Notice that the fact that we *learn* something from painful memories is important here. When we have memories from which we learn nothing, that do nothing other than disturb our peace of mind, or that prevent us from enjoying harmless activities, we may have good reason not to treat them as aspects of ourselves; treating them as foreign forces to be eliminated to the greatest extent possible may well be the best course. Memories of childhood abuse or war that cause post-traumatic stress disorder might fall into this camp. The important fact about such memories is that once you have grown up, or left the war, there is no longer a question about which self is the authority. When it comes to memories like these, it may be that we would be better off having them erased entirely.)

There is a sense, then, in which different emotional memories make you into a different person: Bitter Joel has a very different perspective on the world than Spotless Joel, for example, and will make different decisions. If this is so, then on the picture of agency that requires a single unified decision-making perspective such memories undermine your ability to judge in a profound way, by disrupting your self-conception as a person who has one perspective on the circumstances. On this view, the self is identified with one emotional outlook: memories that overwhelm and distort are outside the boundaries of the self, and many emotions are banished from decision-making. I have been suggesting that we ought to understand what it means to be self-directed in such a way that we can see the various aspects of ourselves as characters we can learn from and learn to work with, more than one of which has the power to help us decide well. On this alternative view, memories bring us in contact with different facets of ourselves; when the memories are distorted, these facets are a part of the self whose role we attempt to limit. We achieve self-direction, on this view, by casting different aspects of the self in different roles (for example, roles such as teacher, student, director) and deciding when there are features that should not be endorsed in any role at all.[13] The metaphor of self-direction as casting-direction helps us recognize that the various aspects of our psychology may not all have the same motivations and interests—they may be different characters—and yet it may be good for us to carve out space in our lives for each of them.

One might think that the view that there are discordant facets of ourselves to be learned from but limited in power is not really very different from a view according to which discordant facets are exiled from the self. What does it matter, for example, if Spotless Joel sees Bitter Joel as an alien force or as part of him? I think that how we see these facets of ourselves does matter, in several ways. First, sometimes it turns out that the bitter, childish, or resentful self is right about something important. Treating those parts of ourselves as exiled monsters precludes taking that point of view seriously anymore.

Second, tolerating the discordant facets of our personality rather than banishing them may, in fact, be a more effective strategy for checking their power in the long run. Emotional responses that are unacknowledged or repressed do often have unfortunate ways of making themselves felt. Interestingly, in the film, Sadder-but-wiser Joel, though emotionally distanced from his memory of the year with Clementine, does not really have the option of disclaiming that perspective as his own. Since he hears his own voice telling the story, he must take this to be *his* reaction. Joel is able to act against that facet of himself because of the emotional distance, while still accepting that this is a part of him.

Finally, how we see these parts of ourselves makes a difference to our ability to sympathize with and understand other people. When I see the bitter, childish, resentful (or whatever) parts of myself as alien monsters that aren't really me, I take no responsibility for them and I am allowed to see myself as a better, more principled person than I really am. I may see myself as overpowered by monsters, but I am permitted to think that this isn't my fault. Unless I extend the same charitable interpretations to other people (which is far from guaranteed), seeing myself in this way can have the effect of making others' behavior look irrational and unprincipled. Learning to tolerate inappropriate aspects of ourselves that do not fit neatly with the rest of our personality may help us be more tolerant of others' idiosyncrasies.

Conclusion

I have argued that painful memories are important to making good judgments because they give us crucial practical information. I have also argued that when painful memories distort the past, which they often do, we need to gain distance from them in some way analogous to the way that Joel does when he learns about his memories from the recording. Finally, I have argued that powerful emotions do not always distort and that when they don't, decisions made from an emotional state of mind may be the best ones. Creating emotional distance only when needed will require us to recognize and manage the multiple perspectives within our own psychology. *Eternal Sunshine of the Spotless Mind* allows us to think about the different aspects of a person and their role in good judgment by presenting us with different versions of the same people, distinguished by what they remember.[14]

Notes

1 Kahneman 1999.
2 Meyer 2008, p. 78.
3 Troy Jollimore (in this volume) suggests that they are doomed in this way even after they have discovered the tapes. David Reeve's essay (also in this volume) leads us to wonder what would be left of Joel and Clem after a memory deletion process, given the way that memories are woven together. If not much of Joel's and Clem's personalities would be left after memory deletion, it may be that they would not repeat their mistakes; however, they also would not really be the same people.
4 Meyer does not say this, nor is he necessarily committed to this view. His main concern is with the disadvantages of the spotless mind; my topic picks up where his left off.
5 Butler 2006 [1726].
6 Damasio 1994.
7 Further, Joel still has the capacity for anger and jealousy. We cannot conclude from the research on brain damaged people that experiences of *particular* emotions such as anger and jealousy are needed for decision-making, only that affective capacity in general is needed, though there is an increasing literature in psychology that aims to establish the motivational role of particular emotions. See note 10.
8 Bell 2005; Spelman 1989.
9 We may not wish that she should literally erase him from her memory, though, since it is instrumentally valuable to know that there are very bad people in the world. (There may be other reasons, too, for not erasing such memories. See Meyer 2008 and Grau 2006.)

10 There is research in psychology to show that emotions such as anger are important moral motivators. For example see Lerner *et al.* 1998. For an overview of the literature on emotions and moral decisions more generally see Tangney *et al.* 2007. This research supports the idea that we may sometimes need to be less distanced from our emotions in order to act appropriately. Thanks to Jesse Prinz for helpful discussion of this topic.

11 Goleman 1995, p. 144.

12 Korsgaard unpublished, p. 15.

13 It might seem that this picture just reduces to the unified agency view by assuming a single, unified casting director. I do not think this is the case. While it is true that decisions about what aspect of the self will play what role must be made, they need not be made by a "decider" who contains no competing forces. Instead, such decisions can be made by whatever constitution of the self is available in the context.

14 I would like to thank Chris Grau, Matt Frank, Mike Rohde, Ian Stoner, and J. D. Walker for helpful comments on previous versions of this paper.

References

Bell, M. (2005) "A woman's scorn: Toward a feminist defense of contempt as a moral emotion," *Hypatia*, 20:4, pp. 80–93.

Butler, J. (2006 [1726]) "Upon Self-Deceit," in David E. White (ed.) *The Works of Bishop Butler* (Rochester, NY: University of Rochester Press), 103–9.

Damasio, A. (1994) *Descartes' Error: Emotion, Reason and the Human Brain* (New York: Grosset/Putnam).

Goleman, D. (1995) *Emotional Intelligence: Why it can matter more than IQ* (New York: Bantam Books).

Grau, C. (2006) "Eternal Sunshine of the Spotless Mind and the Morality of Memory," *Journal of Aesthetics and Art Criticism*, 64:1, pp. 119–33.

Kahneman, D. (1999). "Objective Happiness," in D. Kahneman, E. Diener, and N. Schwarz (eds) *Well-Being: The Foundations of Hedonic Psychology* (New York: Russell Sage Foundation), pp. 3–25.

Korsgaard, C. (unpublished) "Self-Constitution: Action, Identity and Integrity, Lecture One: The Metaphysical Foundations of Normativity."

Lerner, J., Goldberg, J., and Tetlock, P. E. (1998) "Sober Second Thought: The Effects of Accountability, Anger, and Authoritarianism on Attributions of Responsibility," *Personality and Social Psychology Bulletin*, 24, pp. 563–74.

Meyer, Michael J. (2008) "Reflections on Comic Reconciliations: Ethics, Memory, and Anxious Happy Endings," *The Journal of Aesthetics and Art Criticism*, 66:1.

Spelman, E. (1989) "Anger and Insubordination," in A. Gary and M. Pearsall (eds) *Women, Knowledge and Reality: Explorations in Feminist Philosophy* (London and New York: Routledge).

Tangney, J. P., Stuewig, J., and Mashek, D. J. (2007) "Moral Emotions and Moral Behavior," *Annual Review of Psychology*, 58, pp. 345–72.

Chapter 5

Julia Driver

MEMORY, DESIRE, AND VALUE IN *ETERNAL SUNSHINE OF THE SPOTLESS MIND*[1]

IN ETERNAL SUNSHINE CHARLIE KAUFMAN explores the cost of mental peace and tranquility when it comes at the price of authenticity. The plot centers on the issue of voluntary memory purging. A new, rather seedy, business, Lacuna, has opened up and offers clients memory purges that are fairly selective. One can, for example, have the memories of a specific person deleted. Joel Barish decides to have the memories of his relationship with an ex-girlfriend, Clementine Kruczynski, erased. He decides this after finding out that she has had her memories of their relationship erased. His motives are partly reciprocal, but primarily he wants to avoid pain—not only the pain of their relationship but also the pain regarding the knowledge that she erased him from her life. This feature of the plotline in Eternal Sunshine raises a host of extremely interesting ethical issues. We would clearly regard erasing memories non-voluntarily as immoral, as we would taking advantage of the memory loss (as Dr Howard Mierzwiak does with his assistant Mary, and as Stan does with Clementine). But I'm interested in the issue of what we owe people we used to love in terms of memory. My initial reaction when viewing the film was shock that Clementine had done it; and the shock was not just because she is cutting out an important set of memories that reflect part of her life—there was also shock for Joel's sake. Aside from the issue of whether or not it is a good thing for the agent to erase painful memories of a relationship, there arises the issue of whether or not the other person in the relationship has been harmed.[2] I certainly don't want to argue that people ought not to have memories erased—that would be much too radical. But if the other person is harmed, as Joel seems to have been, then that harm would at least have to be weighed in the balance.

The ethics of memory

A good deal of work has already been done on the ethics of memory—often the work relates to the Holocaust, and the issue of whether or not there is a duty to remember others, even when the memories are extraordinarily painful. Some argue "yes"—for example, Avishai Margalit argues that there is a duty that exists at least under certain radical conditions, such as when the shared humanity of persons is attacked, and attacked by profound evil, as happens in genocides.[3] The question, again, that I want to look at is not that of a duty to remember, though the account I suggest certainly has implications for why we would have such a duty. Rather, my focus is whether or not a failure to remember, and, indeed, an active trying to forget, constitutes something bad for the forgotten. Nevertheless, Margalit's framework for his account gives us a useful place to start.

The idea that Margalit has is that memory serves to connect us to others, and is necessary for what he terms "thick" relations. These are the really substantive relationships in our lives, those of love and friendship, for example, as well as those of others we feel connected to, but perhaps to a lesser extent—neighbors and compatriots. What underlies these relationships is caring. Margalit claims that it is caring that is "at the heart of our thick relations."[4] What underlies the caring is memory. He further relies on the distinction between ethics and morality revived by Bernard Williams—ethics is broader, and concerned with living the good life that involves these thick relations—to argue that thick relations are concerned with more than mere morality, more than mere right and wrong. Morality is the sphere of mere right and wrong directed towards others as "bare human beings."[5] I'm skeptical of a distinction between ethics and morality. However, I do believe that some of our relations are "thicker" than others. These are typically the sorts of relations that challenge "impartiality" for those who argue that morality need not be impartial—they give rise to special obligations. In most of the literature these relations are understood as being to specific identifiable individuals, such as a parent's relationship to their child. One of the interesting implications of Margalit's thesis—and potentially problematic—is that some of these relations will be between individuals who don't even know each other, they only know of each other. Indeed, the duty to remember can involve a duty to remember events that happened to a group of others, when one does not know the others in question particularistically. Thus, when Margalit argues that "because it is enmeshed with caring, memory belongs primarily to ethics, not to morality" he is mistaken. One can care about other human beings independently of their particular relationship to oneself. This care underwrites a desire for their well-being, which in turn assumes that the well-being of others is good. Depriving them of this good is a harm. If people desire to be remembered—for whatever reason—then failure to fulfill the desire is a harm (given some qualifications). This does not commit one to a desire-satisfaction view of value. It simply recognizes that one way to harm a person is to fail to fulfill that person's desires, and is compatible with many other types of harm. In *Eternal Sunshine* it is clear that Joel wants to be remembered by Clementine as Clementine's boyfriend, just as Mierzwiak does not want to be remembered by Mary as Mary's lover. Margalit's point that memory underlies our thick relations seems plausible.

Some critics have argued that Margalit is wrong to hold that memory is crucial to thick relations. Galen Strawson, for example, wrote of Margalit's claim:

[A]re actual, explicit memories the cement of thick relations? It sounds attractive, but again I don't think it's generally true. It depends what kind of person you are. Don't worry, reader, if you have a lousy memory, because it doesn't follow that you're no good at thick relations. Michel de Montaigne, famous for his friendship with Etienne de la Boétie, reckoned that he was better at friendship than at anything else, but thought himself ill-equipped to write about memory because "I can find hardly a trace of it in myself; I doubt if there is any other memory in the world as grotesquely faulty as mine is!" When asked why their friendship was as it was, he gave the right answer: because it was him, because it was me. Same with love. Nothing to do with memory.[6]

This seems too strong. Margalit's thesis is compatible with the view that one needn't remember every single detail of a past experience of a person in order to live up to the duty to remember. Of course, how detailed the memory should be is open to more reflection. But if the relationships are special due to their caring nature, then a place to start would be to require the relevant memories to be the ones that underlie the caring. One needn't remember that the loved one wore a red shirt to the party, only that he was there with you and you had a good time. So, some memories will be more significant when it comes to underlying the thick relationships that Margalit discusses.

Note, too, there is an overtone of respect to this sort of caring. One owes it to those who are gone or absent. And this is precisely the direction I want to explore in this paper. My focus is not on the issue of memory's significance to personal identity and its value in preserving personal identity. Much of the philosophical interest in films with a "memory disruption" theme has centered on how the disruption of an individual's memory either does or does not change that person into a wholly new individual. This topic is very interesting, but my focus is on how memory *benefits* others. This is why the caring that Margalit discusses really needs to be viewed as *positive* caring. If the caring were instead simply viewed as caring in *some way or other*, even in a *negative* way, the claim would lose all plausibility. There may be people in one's life who have been vicious, nasty, and utterly destructive. One may still care about them in the sense that one is interested in what happens to them. But one doesn't, and maybe oughtn't, desire their well-being. The caring that underlies the thick relationships will, I take it, be positive, however, where one desires the well-being of the one who is cared for.

This seems quite plausible. An amnesic would be lost and alone. Memories are what tie us to the past and what underlie our sense of duty and reciprocity. Without the memory of a favor, one would not feel gratitude. Without the memory of harm, one would not feel appropriate resentment. Some of these emotions are negative, and painful, but still serve a useful purpose in focusing our thoughts on things we know to be avoided. In that way, Clementine's erasure of her memories of Joel may not be good, even by her own lights, as she is having them removed. In the end, she and Joel are drawn back together. Maybe it's well worth it—and certainly Joel's experience with Lacuna shows that he thought, in the end, before the memories were completely stripped, that it *was* well worth it. It is with memory that one can decide whether it is worth it or not. Without the memory one is left without the information. And at the conclusion of the film, after Mary has sent the tapes to Lacuna's patients, Joel and Clementine have some of the information back, though with less intensity than they would have had with the actual memory. The film concludes with the implication that even though it wasn't spotless, the relationship was still precious. Given some of the Nietzschean references in the film as well, there is almost a sense of its inevitability. But it's the loss of memory that would result in that "eternal recurrence," not a cosmic recurrence of the physical events leading up to the relationship. If one can't remember the previous relationship, there is no choice to *repeat* it, and all its mistakes, in the present world. And one doesn't even realize that there is repetition. When Mierzwiak's assistant Mary sends the tapes of the procedures to his patients, Joel and Clementine have the choice returned to them. Certainly people want to be remembered, especially by those who are important to them. Evidence for this is that we apologize and feel bad when we've forgotten someone we feel we ought to remember—an old high school friend, for example. The apology indicates that there is something to apologize for, and feel bad *about*. In these sorts of cases it's an indication to the other person that they just weren't significant enough to remember, that you didn't care enough to remember. And this is just a case of passive memory loss. When the memory loss is intended, the harm, if there is harm, must be worse. We can see this by looking at typical reactive attitudes. When a harm is unintentional the harmed person is upset, but when the harm is intended the harmed person feels anger and resentment directed towards the person who harmed them.

Memory is important, too, when it comes to providing relevant information for practical deliberation—information about oneself and others. Again, the amnesic would be at a loss when it comes to a certain type of prudential reasoning. How can one work to achieve one's life goal if one cannot remember what it is? In the case of the amnesic, what seems to be prudential is a kind of mental archeology—trying to figure out what one's goals *were*, to fill in the memory gaps. The agent's perspective in practical deliberation is impersonal rather than timeless; there is a switch from prudence to altruism.[7] "Practical deliberation" refers to the sort of deliberation agents make use of in deciding how to *act*. Thus it involves "practical" rather than "theoretical" reason. Intuitively, there are two types of practical deliberation: (1) prudential, which employs self-regarding reasons, or those that reflect one's own well-being; and (2) moral, which employs other-regarding reasons, and often expresses a concern for the well-being of others. But if one can't remember one's own goals, one loses a grip on what counts as a prudential reason, and instead one regards the self as a kind of other person for whom one has to discover goals to help satisfy. It reflects the way one regards time-slices of the self—as really part of the self, or as another person whose interests are intimately con-nected to one, but only causally. In his discussion of prudence and altruism Nagel notes that people can take different stances and consider different sorts of reasons in practical deliberation. The timeless reasons are the ones underlying prudence. The stance where one considers the timeless reasons in practical deliberation is one where the agent considers the present time as only one time among many others in their life. The stance of altruism is the stance where one considers impersonal reasons—where one considers oneself as one person among others in the world. Of course, these impersonal and timeless reasons come into play when we consider other cases of altruism. When one considers the *future* well-being of *others* as opposed to the self, the reasons will be both. Their future is a time, among other times, just as their lives are lives among other lives including the agent's own. In the case of Joel and Clementine, when they look at the tapes at the end of the film, and review what happened, they are getting back information. But they are taking the impersonal stance. Joel sees someone he, in effect, has no first-person knowledge of.

Of course, in the film, Joel is told about his past with Clementine via Mary's revelations. So he knows that the man in love with Clementine was himself. But instead of knowing via memory, he knows via a description of a situation he used to remember. It is like the knowledge of the past someone gets looking through a very old photo album. "That was *me* in the picture playing with the kitten, but I have no memory of it." Thus, Joel has information about his past, but no first-person knowledge of it, since he is lacking the memory of it.

The loss of the first-person perspective can't simply be reduced to loss of information. The tapes provide information. Indeed, it is even possible that watching the tapes gives one higher quality, more reliable, information about one's past life. Rather, the special quality has to do with the causal chain, and how one is cognizant of that information. One reason is that lack of memory is sometimes taken to indicate lack of care, or feeling. One might feel vaguely guilty for failing to remember the name of someone, for example, because it might be seen to indicate that when one met the person one couldn't be bothered to remember his name.

First-person knowledge, the actual memory, then, is extremely important in how we appreciate the experience of *recalling* information. Here is a thought experiment: Rob suffers a head injury in a skiing accident. He wakes up in the hospital. He remembers nothing about his past. However, he believes the woman who talks to him and tells him that she is his wife, and he believes the two children who come to visit him are his children, though he doesn't remember them. His wife shows him extensive home movies, and he comes to know certain things about what he did in the past, and so on. He has lots of information, and lots of knowledge, though it is not first-person. His physician tells him that a new procedure would restore his memory, though it would be costly. How much would he be willing to pay, nevertheless, to get the memories back? Probably quite a bit. His family would want him to do it as well. So more than having just the information about the past, memory seems to carry with it certain emotional connections that are valuable. Losing those is a real harm, then. The same kind of a sense of loss is reflected in the character at the end of *Memento* who knows abstractly that he has had his revenge, but really wants the first-person memory of it, to savor it and fully appreciate it.

So, off hand, one might propose that first-person experience that is recalled in memory has much more vivacity to it than mere propositional memory, which is memory of the information of one's past. Propositional memory is memory of learning the proposition that contains information, and here is used in contrast with memory that is essentially experiential rather than memory of learning a particular proposition. I can remember having propositional knowledge conveyed to me—as when Joel watches the video that provides information to him about his past, and then later remembers that information—but recalling the information is not the same as having experienced the state of affairs in question. So, my belief that I was a cute baby, for example, is based on my memory of my mother telling me "You were a cute baby," not memory of my cuteness itself.

Our ordinary reaction to failures to remember indicates that there is something in a failure to remember that is bad. But is it harmful to the person who has been forgotten? For example, one could argue that the failure itself is not bad but is evidence of the person's failure to care— that is, evidence of a character failure. I think in many cases that's what is going on. But it doesn't capture the full story—the case above, where the skier loses his memory, shows that its badness must at least to some extent be linked to some other consideration or set of considerations since the skier, Rob, did not choose to lose his memory. It happened to him. He was just unlucky rather than morally deficient in some way that is reflected in his memory.

One possibility that seems promising is that when someone has lost his memory of loved ones it affects the way he cares about them, if he cares about them at all. We need to use the distinction between *de re* and *de dicto* belief and desire to make this point salient. For example, desire *de re* is a desire for something specific or particular. Desire *de dicto* is a general unspecific desire. One example used by Quine is "I want a sloop." Read *de dicto*, the subject simply wants to have some sloop or other. Read *de re* the subject wants a specific sloop.[8]

Now consider our case of the skier again. When he wakes up in the hospital and is told he has a wife and children, the following can be said of him:

(1) Rob believes that he is married and has children.

On a *de dicto* reading of this, Rob believes that he is married to someone or other, and has some children, though he doesn't know who they are. He simply believes that the proposition "I have a wife and children" is true. On a *de re* reading he believes that he is married to a particular person, *Maria*, and that belief carries with it a range of specific beliefs about Maria. The emotions attached to each belief will be different. When Rob first wakes up, his belief is *de dicto*. Rob may also have a desire to be a good husband to his wife, and at first this desire is *de dicto* as well. He as yet has no desire to be a good husband specifically *to Maria*, particularly since he lacks specific knowledge of Maria's likes and dislikes, and can only form the most general beliefs about what he ought to do in being a good husband.[9] Michael Smith noted in his discussion of moral motivation that we think of good persons as being motivated not by abstractions (i.e. "I desire to do the right thing, whatever it is") but by something more substantive and rich—by particular non-derivative right-making considerations (i.e. "I desire to do it because it's kind"). If a person, in his view, is motivated by desire *de dicto*, then she is alienated "from the ends at which morality properly aims."[10] Similarly, Rob's wife will feel distressed to learn that he doesn't remember her, even knowing that he has told his doctor he wants to be a good husband. She knows it's not the right kind of desire upon which to have the kind of relationship that involves love and commitment to a particular person. With that level of emotional commitment stripped out, the relationship is very much lacking. Of course, over time, there will be the shift from *de dicto* to *de re*.

This move is similar to that made by Robert Kraut, who employs the *de dicto/de re* distinction to try to account for how we love *particularistically*.[11] That is, when we love someone, that person is irreplaceable in our love— love is focused on the particular individual, and not on similar objects. Indeed, it is taken to be incompatible with true love if Jennie loves Jeff and anyone similar to Jeff. Loving Jeff rules out the love of someone in particular who is very similar to Jeff when Jennie's history is informed only by the experiences she has with Jeff, rather than the person similar to Jeff.[12] Kraut notes that, on one theory of how we name objects using proper names, or names that refer to particular individuals or objects, those names refer in such a way that they can't shift over to other objects, even very similar ones. This kind of designation is called "rigid designation." So, for example, when a particular baby is born, let's say that her parents dub her "Alice Smith." She and no one else is that Alice Smith. If someone refers to her as "Sarah Smith," that person is mistaken. If someone refers to her clone as "Alice Smith," that person is mistaken as well. The clone may be like Alice, but the clone is not Alice. Kraut exploits this feature of naming in an analogy with love—love has that same non-transferable quality to it.

In the case of Rob, over time, as desire goes from *de dicto* to *de re* desire with respect to the particular individuals in his family, he will get a lessening of that feeling of alienation from the thick relationships that are such an important part of his life. But it probably will not ever go away completely as long as he fails to remember. So this won't fully explain the problem. However, it does give a way to unpack Margalit's insight. What Margalit terms "thick" relationships—spousal, parental, and so forth—are relationships to particular people that one is connected to by one's first-person experiences, some of those being memories of events that form a part of the relationships. These provide the basis for the beliefs and desires that influence how the relationships are understood in the present and how they are to develop in the future. The sorts of reasons one needs to be responsive to have a desire *de re* are "thick" ones—particular to the event or individual. What one is lacking in a good thick relationship, then, is *mere* desire *de dicto*, or *only* desire *de dicto*. In the case of our amnesic, Rob, he can begin *again* accumulating those first-person experiences and memories, and thus *de dicto* transforms into *de re*, but at the start his connection to the ones that he is told he cares about does not qualify.

It is really clear that this state of affairs is a misfortune for Rob, but it is also a misfortune for his wife and children. They want something they don't have, and that, as his family, they are entitled to. The harm they suffer, then, is tied to their desires. This means that being forgotten is not always a bad thing for the person who is forgotten. Someone may want to be forgotten, because he's in danger, or he thinks he won't be remembered fondly, or for any number of reasons. We see this at work in *Eternal Sunshine* in the form of Howard Mierzwiak. He does not want Mary to remember their relationship. He rationalizes this by appealing to the pain it caused her and the recurring pain the memories of it would cause her. But, as with Joel and Clementine, she is more likely to repeat the painful error if she doesn't remember having made the same mistake before. And note that Mierzwiak keeps his memory of the relationship, and puts himself in a position that the audience is invited to infer is completely morally bankrupt because he is in a position to take advantage of her crush, based on her new ignorance, yet again. He changes her contempt into adoration and he does so without having to change *himself*.

Other examples will involve more than embarrassment but actual hatred. Sophia may hate Constance to the point where she would love it if Constance completely forgot her. The satisfaction of that desire is then good for Sophia. But it's interesting to point out that this isn't always the case when one hates somebody. Some thick relations involve hatred— deep and abiding hatred. Revenge, for example, may involve the desire to be remembered by the person revenged upon. As in the *Memento* case— not only would the agent like to remember, he would also like to *be* remembered as the agent of his enemy's suffering.

A memory has to have the right kind of causal history. In *Blade Runner* engineered humans could have implanted "memories" that were actually, for them, pseudo-memories. These "memories" would not have the same value as genuine memories even if they had exactly the same feel as genuine memories. As with our other experiences, there is a preference for the veridical.

So far we've been considering cases of very personal sorts of remembering, remembering as a two-person relation—x is remembered by y; or even e in x's life is remembered by y.

There is a more open-ended sort of desire that some have—the desire to be remembered, though not by a specifically identifiable individual or set of individuals. Notice that here the desire is *de dicto*—one desires to be remembered by someone or other, but there's nothing specific about the identity. This desire is what motivates people to have their names put on buildings and scholarship funds. This is not motivated the same way as the other desires we've discussed. Joel desires that Clementine cares for him, even if the care is tinged with feelings such as exasperation. The non-specific *de dicto* desire of the donor is for something like future, long-term appreciation. He or she desires to be known as someone who made a positive difference. Though it would be misleading to call this kind of memory as important to "thick" relationships, it is this kind of memory that in part underlies discussions of duties to remember the past. *We* may have a duty to remember the past, but that duty is not based on the desire of those people in the past to be remembered. I take it that Margalit would argue that even if they had no such desire, we would still have a duty to remember some past events in individuals' lives since those events are important in understanding social bonds. This is compatible with the approach I articulate here, since I have no intention of holding that the desire-satisfaction is exhaustive of value. Further, the "we" in this claim is vague. It seems that most of the time what's important is that there is a cultural memory of the past embodied in the present institutions—such as schools, museums, etc.

I have been arguing that failure to remember someone is harmful to that person under certain circumstances, such as when the agent desires to be remembered. This has the appearance of plausibility, and I have tried to explain what specifically is at work in such putative harms. But a critic might argue that in spite of the appearance of plausibility it is in fact just false. Consider the Parfit-style cases where, let's say, Rob has a desire to be remembered five thousand years into the future.[13] But five thousand years after his death no one remembers Rob. Has he been harmed? Parfit notes that on what he terms a Success theory, Rob will be harmed by this only if the desire was crucial to the way he lived his life in some way—if, for example, he worked hard to ensure that he is remembered in the distant future, by constructing big, solid, erosion-resistant monuments to himself, for example. If the desire deeply figured in how he led his life, and it was something he very, very deeply cared about, it does seem as though Rob has been harmed. If, on the other hand, Rob has the desire but it is not something that is really operational for him—it doesn't structure how he lives his life, etc.—then intuitively it does not seem that he has been harmed by the failure of the desire to be satisfied.

We can use this in articulating a plausible account of why Joel is harmed in *Eternal Sunshine*. The way in which the desire goes unfulfilled is also relevant. If Rob truly has a desire to be remembered five thousand years from now, and this desire is *operational* rather than passive, then it does seem that Rob is harmed by a failure to remember, even though no specific individual has harmed him. This would be on analogy with a person who has been harmed by a failure to receive charity, even though no specific individual has harmed him. But if the desire is passive rather than operational, he has not been harmed. The desire is one that has not shaped his life, his plans, his projects.

Conclusion

When persons, as they often do, have a desire to be remembered, failure to remember them constitutes a harm to them. This is independent of the issue of whether or not we have an obligation to remember them, or the past, more generally. It may be that we have an obligation to remember even if others are harmed. It may be that we have no obligation to remember even if others are harmed. Separate arguments would have to be made, and my view on these issues is that it will depend on the balance of benefits and harms in a given case. But irrespective of the obligation issue, failure to remember—when it conflicts with a desire—can thereby constitute a harm to the person who wants to be remembered. Sometimes this is very specific—x desires to be remembered by y. Sometimes it is open ended—x desires to be remembered in a more open-ended sort of way. This memory is not something that underlies thick relations except in a very derivative sort of way, by supporting institutions that improve quality of life, which in turn enhance thick relations (as well as simple individual well-being). When a desire that figures into the nitty-gritty of an agent's practical deliberations in life—an operational desire—goes unfulfilled, the agent has experienced a harm. The agent in such cases may or may not have been harmed by a specific individual. Clearly, in the case of Joel Barish, he has been harmed by Clementine's willful erasure of him from her mind. Again, this is completely independent of whether or not she has an obligation to remember him. We know from the film that Joel desired that Clementine remember him, and that his relationship with Clementine was incredibly important to him. After he finds out about what she did, he goes to her. His subsequent behavior, his attempt to erase her from his mind and to eliminate those desires by eliminating memories of her, can be seen as an attempt to eliminate or cancel out the harm she did him. But what Joel discovered as he was losing those memories was that he didn't really want to eliminate the harm, at least not in that way. There is a little bit something of bad faith, perhaps, in excising a desire like love rather than letting experience transform it. Losing a limb is bad, but then making yourself not want the leg anymore may not be the right sort of response to the harm.

Notes

1 I would like to thank Carl Craver and Christopher Grau for helpful comments on earlier versions of the paper. Some of the material in this paper was presented at a talk to the Philosophy Department at the University of New Hampshire in Spring 2008. I would like to thank the members of the Department and their students for a great discussion.

2 Many authors on the ethics of memory tend to focus on the first issue—that is, how losing memory can diminish the quality of one's life. See Michael Meyer's discussion of this in relation to Eternal Sunshine of the Spotless Mind in Meyer 2008, pp. 77–87.
3 Margalit 2003.
4 Margalit 2003, p. 37.
5 Margalit 2003.
6 Strawson 2003, a review of The Ethics of Memory.
7 See Nagel 1979.
8 Quine 1956, pp. 177–87.
9 I here follow Michael Smith's use of the desire de re and desire de dicto distinction. See Smith 1994.
10 Smith 1994, p.76.
11 Kraut 1986, pp. 413–30.
12 This is debatable. A recent episode of Doctor Who has Rose arguably in love with the Doctor's humanized replica.
13 Parfit 1986. See the discussion of various factors that make a life go well, particularly discussion of the Success theory, pp. 149 ff.

References

Kraut, Robert (1986) "Love De Re," in Peter A. French, Theodore E. Uehling, and Howard K. Wettstein (eds) Midwest Studies in Philosophy, Vol. X, Minneapolis, MN: University of Minnesota Press, pp. 413–30.

Margalit, Avishai (2003) The Ethics of Memory, Cambridge, MA: Harvard University Press.

Meyer, Michael (2008) "Reflections on Comic Reconciliations: Ethics, Memory, and Anxious Happy Endings," The Journal of Aesthetics and Art Criticism, Winter, pp. 77–87.

Nagel, Thomas (1979) The Possibility of Altruism, New York: Princeton University Press.

Parfit, Derek (1986) Reasons and Persons, Oxford: Oxford University Press.

Quine, W. V. O. (1956) "Quantifiers and Propositional Attitudes," Journal of Philosophy, March 1, pp. 177–87.

Smith, Michael (1994) The Moral Problem, Oxford: Blackwell.

Strawson, Galen (2003) "Blood and Memory," The Guardian, January 4.

Chapter 6

Stephen L. White

MICHEL GONDRY AND THE PHENOMENOLOGY OF VISUAL PERCEPTION

The camera analogy

A NUMBER OF MAJOR FILM THEORIES, particularly those of André Bazin and such later figures as Christian Metz and Noël Burch, involve a set of explicit and implicit assumptions about film, space, and visual perception, including:

1   The photographic image is the product of a process of mechanical reproduction. Hence it is an objective record or trace of the objects and events depicted.

2   Because the mechanical nature of photographic reproduction precludes interpretation or bias, the photographic image has a privileged representational relation to space and to the physical objects and events it contains.

3   Film is, in its essence, a sequence of such images or shots joined to form significant narrative or temporal wholes. The creative contribution of the filmmaker lies in the selection of such images or shots and in the construction of such sequences, not in the construction or manipulation of the images themselves.[1]

Such claims allow and support the idea that the physical space depicted in film is a construction. Such depiction is a matter of the juxtaposition of shots that, viewed sequentially, are seen as presenting appropriately related parts of a space that is single, homogeneous, and unified. A shot, for example, of a person opening a door followed by a shot from inside as that person enters a room will be seen as depicting adjacent parts of a single, uniform space, regardless of how far removed from one another the actual spaces may be. That the space depicted is a construction, however, is true, according to the theorists in question, only for the space outside the individual film frames. What is given inside the frame is assumed to be an unconstructed and unmanipulated—hence objective and unbiased—representation. According to Bazin, this conception of the photograph as an unmediated physical trace that the past leaves in the present makes it more analogous to a death mask or a footprint than to a painted portrait. (In addition to being central to the film theories in question, this is a conception that recurs in much of the writing on still photography, including that of Susan Sontag and Roland Barthes.)[2] The upshot is that the manipulation or construction of the images themselves is, on Bazin's view, illegitimate. As a consequence, film practices involving such artistic manipulation of the image itself—including German expressionism, Russian experiments with montage, the French and American avant-garde traditions, and animation—have often been marginalized in the context of theoretical discussion.

   The assumptions of such film theories have their counterparts in a philosophical conception of visual perception—a conception that runs through the empiricist theories of the seventeenth and eighteenth centuries and their twentieth century descendant, the sense-datum theory.[3] According to these theories, what we are given most immediately and directly in visual perception are not external physical objects but image-like mental entities that, though they exist only "before the mind's eye," bear a strong analogy to the images that the external world projects on the retina. Thus a white cup viewed in red light will produce (in a normal subject) a red sense-datum. A round plate viewed at an angle will produce a sense-datum that is literally elliptical in shape. And two identical objects viewed at different distances will produce sense-data that are literally different in size. On this theory, only such apparent colors, shapes, and relative sizes can be given in visual perception directly and without conscious inference. Moreover, because of the analogies between retinal and photographic images, sense-data are taken to be analogous to both. And because of the appeal in both cases to mechanical metaphors for the process whereby the image is produced, visual experience, like photographic reproduction, is assumed to be largely neutral and objective —that is, largely free of interpretation and bias.

Michel Gondry's films challenge the assumptions of both these film theories and the philosophical theories of perception. In many of Gondry's films, the most important artistic contributions consist not in the linking of shots, but in the manipulation, construction, or creation of the image within the frame. These films, I shall argue, make us aware of the nature of perception under a number of fundamental human forms and categories and in terms of a number of humanly significant distinctions. The categories include time, causation, and intentionality, and the relevant distinctions include inside/outside, private/public, and self/ other. Such perception reveals on analysis that what we see, both on the screen and in ordinary perception, is anything but a homogeneous space, mechanically and transparently given. Rather, it is a patchwork of zones and boundaries, traces and signs, as haunted as the screen by an expressionist film and as full of incommensurabilities as a list by Borges or Greenaway.

That Gondry challenges the standard assumptions about film, space, and perception is most apparent in his music videos and short films. I believe, however, that *Eternal Sunshine of the Spotless Mind*, though ostensibly conventional in its treatment of space and time, must be viewed in the context of Gondry's more radical experiments. Viewed in this light,

Eternal Sunshine is a kind of negative image of his short films, the richness of whose images suggests a kind of visual perception that far exceeds what the camera analogy would allow as the apprehension of properties given directly. What *Eternal Sunshine* depicts, by contrast, is the dismantling of that rich life-world of highly structured, partially interpenetrating, and partially incommensurable zones of meaning and functionality. The result is the experience of an impoverished world, the product of the "brain damage" implicit in the artificial elimination of memories. As objects, places, and associations disappear, the space surrounding Joel, the main character, comes to resemble an empty stage, and we are reminded of the richness of normal perception by the contrast with its artificially depleted opposite. Far from giving us transparent access to an uninterpreted world as both the sense-datum theory and the film theories under consideration require, we are given, I shall argue, a world of opportunities for meaningful action and engagement—a world with respect to which our perception is anything but passive and one that bears little resemblance to the theatrical and spectatorial space that gave the seventeenth and eighteenth centuries their most potent metaphor for perception—that of the experience of a detached spectator, either of a theatrical performance or of the images created in the camera obscura.

Optical traces

Gondry's bringing to the fore the complex structure of our lived space most often involves reversals of our normal expectations. This technique of illuminating a phenomenon by presenting its antithesis recurs frequently in Gondry's most subtle meditations on visual perception: his reflections on the principles on the basis of which space and time may be interchanged. That Gondry is preoccupied with the ways in which the past leaves visible traces in the present is made clear in an interview about the making of one of his music videos, The Chemical Brothers' *Let Forever Be*. As one of the artists for whom it was made put it, "I was imagining it more as kind of video effects and like trails and traces and stuff and then he came up with the idea that the effects would be real . . ."[4]

But what is a trace, and where is it located? In the interview, traces are associated with optical effects that produce the visual equivalent of echoes or reverberations. Gondry explores a variety of such effects.

In one kind of optical effect— a multiple exposure—past moments leave their traces directly on the film image itself. In the music video *Come into My World*, Kylie Minogue walks approximately the same path along and across city streets several times. Each time she makes a complete circuit, she is joined by her earlier self, who retraces the earlier path while she herself takes a slightly different route. This is an optical effect in some respects comparable to the clichéd effect of long exposures in still photography that turn what would be images of headlights and taillights at night in a short exposure into extended trajectories that trace the cars' routes in space over extended periods.

Multiple exposures may involve the printing within one frame of images that purport to be of the same time. Fairly recent examples include the split-screen sequences in Alexander Payne's *Sideways*. Multiple exposures may also include images that purport to be of different times. (In Peter Greenaway's *The Pillow Book*, which is a compendium of such techniques, there is a screen split into nine portions, in each of which we see a stage in the production of a book.) Moreover, the relations between the different exposures in the same frame can vary widely. They may be simultaneous views from different perspectives of the same scene (*Sideways*), or simultaneous views of different scenes involving related characters (Mike Figgis's *Timecode*, in which the screen is divided into four parts for the duration of the film). In *Come into My World*, the most important examples are images of Kylie Minogue at different times corresponding to the same stage of the different circuits around her route. And in Gondry's multiply split-screen video for Jean-François Cohen, *La Tour de Pise*, temporal relations between the static images are largely irrelevant. Nor does temporality normally figure in cases when images are printed over one another because of a similarity of two-dimensional shape and an analogical or other meaning relation. The screen may also be divided to produce a picture within a picture, as are many of the shots in *The Pillow Book*. And cases of words on the screen, as in the famous image in Robert Wiene's *The Cabinet of Dr Caligari*, provide another kind of example.

Come into My World, however, involves a second optical technique besides multiple exposure—the (possibly multiple) reproduction of the same exposure. During each circuit, we see Kylie's earlier circuits reproduced to accompany the circuit we are seeing in the present. Of course, the simplest and purest example of such reproduction is the freeze

frame. In another example, some structuralist films of the 1970s inter-
polated between each pair of frames multiple reproductions to produce
an effect of motion so slow as to be almost imperceptible. Film loops,
of which there are a number in Gondry's work, provide another type of
example, as do slow motion instant replays. And flash forwards that are
later reproduced in their more complete, present-tense contexts play a
significant narrative role in Nicolas Roeg's *Don't Look Now*.

Some of the most interesting cases of multiple exposures within a
frame and of the reproduction of exposures within one or several frames
are those that combine both techniques. What we might call "trails" or
"echoes" provide one obvious example. In this case, an image (exposure)
in one frame is reproduced in a number of subsequent frames—not
necessarily every one—as are subsequent images, while the object pro-
ducing the images moves across the screen. The result can be a continuous
trail behind the object like that of a shooting star or the vapor trail of an
airplane. Alternatively, it can be a blurred but not fully continuous trail
more strictly analogous to what we see in many futurist paintings.
This latter technique is used effectively by Norman McLaren, an
acknowledged influence on Gondry, in *Pas de Deux*. A somewhat similar
use occurs in the stylized sword fight shown in close up and chiaroscuro
in the credit sequence of Richard Lester's *The Three Musketeers*. Such multi-
plications of an image within the frame, however, needn't be limited
to traces of the trajectories of past motion. Images can multiply or
"reverberate" in any direction or outward in all directions. And, of course,
such images can be multiplied according to any formal pattern, some of
which, including kaleidoscopic effects, have become virtual clichés.

Traces in the world

The relevance to Gondry of this catalogue does not lie primarily in his
use of such effects but in the startling way in which he calls attention to
them. In so doing, he calls into question their implications for the
interconnections of space and time and our perceptions and representa-
tions of these fundamental forms of experience. Gondry brings such easily
produced optical effects to our attention by photographing real physical
objects so as to produce an identical film image. By doing so—with great
ingenuity and often at considerable trouble and expense—Gondry invites
us to reflect on the different ways in which the past is given to us in its

traces in the present. And this is a (or the) major theme not only of many of his short films and music videos but also of *Eternal Sunshine of the Spotless Mind*.

The simplest version of this transformation of the optical into the real occurs in Gondry's music video, *The Hardest Button to Button*. Gondry produces the effect of rapidly multiplying images of a drum set, with the drummer seated at the drum on the leading edge of the sequence—a sequence timed to the beat of the music. What could have been done optically, or now digitally, is accomplished by stop-action animation and the use of thirty-two identical sets of drums. It is in The Chemical Brothers' video *Let Forever Be*, however, that some of Gondry's most ingenious re-creations occur. In this video, Gondry photographs real objects to produce such effects as kaleidoscopic imagery, mirrors receding to infinity, multiple, synchronized images of the actress (using six look-alikes), two-dimensional patterning (using actresses with flat cardboard masks posed among pasteboard stage sets), and so forth. The suggestion of a dialectical interplay between the optical and the real is reinforced when we recall the explicit interplay between optically produced doubles and a real physical double in Norman McLaren's *Narcissus*.

In a number of other films Gondry explores the borderline between optically produced imagery and equivalent images of three-dimensional space—or between traces of the past on film and traces in the world. In *Eternal Sunshine*, the elongated dent in Joel's car is another real-world spatial counterpart of the optically produced traces of past motion. And like the optical trails in the Lester film, the dent is a record of a trajectory of motion—in this case, the motion of the car relative to the fire hydrant valve that produced it. And in many traces of trajectories, we "read through" the trace to the past events. This is a fact frequently exploited by still photographers to produce a rich experiential and visual sense of the past that is always implicit in the photographic image.

Suppose we accept that many of the Gondry videos and short films invite us to reflect on the different ways in which the past leaves its traces in the present, both on film and in the world. What is the significance of this for our understanding of *Eternal Sunshine*, if, as I suggested, it is a negative image of the shorter works? *Eternal Sunshine* differs from those works in two respects. First, the full-length film is concerned exclusively with physical traces of the past (including those in memory), as opposed to its traces on film. Second, the contrast in *Eternal Sunshine* is not primarily between traces on film and their real-world counterparts. And this is true even though some scenes could have been done more easily as trick photography and so call attention to the distinction. (The scenes of Joel as a small child under the table and bathing in a sink are obvious examples). Rather, the contrast is between physical traces and the lack of such traces, particularly as a result of their erasure. Ultimately it is a contrast designed to reveal the difference between a world saturated with the past, with memory—a world that is an external memory—and one devoid of such significance.

Physical traces serve first and foremost to orient us in the narrative of a relationship—a narrative that is unfolding in reverse. The change in Clementine's hair color from orange to blue occurs shortly after the end of her relationship with Joel, and it serves to distinguish their first trip to the Charles from the second. The elongated dent in Joel's car occurs just before their break-up. Joel's collecting and relinquishing the objects and journal pages associated with Clementine occurs in the afternoon before the erasure of his memories, hence the day before Valentine's Day. His discovery of the nearly empty whisky bottle in his kitchen occurs at a later time than the erasure of his memories. The tapes of their interviews at the clinic come into Joel's and Clementine's possession after Mary learns of her affair with Dr Mierzwiak and the erasure of her own memories, etc. We infer, then, a coherent timeline for the narrative on the basis of (among other things) such traces.

Expression

But the influence of the past on the present is also subtler and more immediately relevant to the way in which past events can be given in perception. Sex between Stan and Mary seems frenetic and sad, though it has a briefly touching moment while they are asleep together in a chair. (The moment foreshadows Mary's later reference to the innocent baby, unburdened by memory and sadness.) Mary's drinking seems compulsive and aimed at dulling a present haunted by past pain. Her relation with Stan is an echo of her relation with Dr Mierzwiak. And we see the sadness of the expressions of Mary and Dr Mierzwiak and the sadness and anger of his wife as Mary learns of the earlier relationship.

It is common to talk of seeing such sadness—less common to take such talk as literally true. But the sadness of the characters is not something we infer on the basis of their expressions or behavior. We are given the sadness directly by looking *through* the expressions. And the most specific thing we can normally say about the expressions or behavior we have seen is that they are sad.

What is true of sadness, I believe, is true of the past. We see the past pain suffused through the present, and, thus, the past in the present. And the reasons are both philosophical and phenomenological. When Clementine meets Joel after their memories of each other have been erased, she tells him he looks familiar. This is a very ordinary experience and seemingly a perceptual one. In this case and in general it appears that there is nothing else in which the experience could consist. Certainly in many normal cases the thought that one has seen a person before seems to be the result of the way the person looks. And in Clementine's case there is nothing besides the perceptual experience that could motivate and make intelligible such a thought.

But what does something look like when it looks familiar? Most of us have had the experience of seeing something like a park in a strange city and then seeing it again, much later, from the same position and angle when the layout of the city and the location and orientation of the park have become familiar. The park looks different, but in no way that a camera could capture or a painting represent. This in itself is a strong reason for abandoning the camera analogy and the pictorial conception of visual perceptual experience.

The alternative, as I shall argue, is a theory according to which what we are given directly in visual perception is both more and less than the sense-datum theory allows.[5] We are given more in that we perceive such features of the world as causal relations, such functional properties as the property an object has in virtue of being useful in certain ways, such value-laden properties as someone or something's being intriguing, attractive, or inspiring, and such expressive properties as another person's being angry, sad, or distressed. However, we are also given less than the sense-datum theory requires. When we see that a friend is distressed, we are often given our friend's distress directly, and not as the result of an inference based on anything more basic that we are given in visual perception. We are not, for example, typically aware of the subtle features of our friend's facial geometry in virtue of which the distress is given to us visually—much less are we aware of the sense-data on the basis of which the facial geometry is given. And this is no more mysterious than the fact that we may be given a word without being consciously aware of the typeface or the fact that in a fast-paced conversation with several speakers using a number of different languages, we may be unaware of the language being used while we are concentrating on the idea being expressed.

Causation and functionality

In saying that the experience of someone as familiar is perceptual, we are saying that some aspect of the past is implicit in the perceptual content of the experience and not merely inferred from it. This may seem to fall short of the claim that the past can be given in perception. Here, again, however, Gondry's shorter films are relevant. Time is implicit in motion and causation, and Gondry calls our attention to causation in a wide variety of examples in the Beck video, *Deadweight*. Causality and agency are reversed in shots of Beck's shoes walking in front of him and of a man carrying a car. A similar reversal occurs in the shots of Beck's shadow walking upright, dragging Beck horizontally along the sidewalk behind him. Beck takes clothes out of his drawer, and after a quick shake they are mysteriously folded and ready to pack. Beck's shadow makes a phone call on which he eavesdrops, and so forth. There is also a pervasive pattern of causal connections between events in the Beck narrative and events in the scenes from *A Life Less Ordinary*, with which that narrative is intercut. A man on the beach throws a toy car in the direction of the water, and a real car crashes down an embankment. Beck is knocked down, and we see Ewan McGregor on the ground, having been wrestled down by several policemen. A boy on the beach plays with toy cars almost causing a collision in front of a modern building sculpted in the sand, and the same events are played out with real cars in front of a downtown building. Beck has handles attached to the front of his suit jacket, which he starts to open, and Ewan McGregor opens a satchel full of money with a similar pair of handles. In addition, there are the many reversals of time in Gondry's feature length film, *The Science of Sleep*. Stephane invents a "one-second time machine," and in one scene, water flows backwards. These reversals are closely tied to the reversals of the direction of causation in the Beck video and parallel the reversed narrative of *The Eternal Sunshine of the Spotless Mind* and the complete reversal of the film in the music video of Cibo Matto's *Sugar Water*.

Many functional relations are also reversed in the Beck video. These include functional zones normally given as an inside and outside separated by a boundary—wallpaper appears inside a picture frame, and the picture covers the whole wall, reminding us of the distinction between the space inside and outside the film frame. In other instances, the two exteriors of two such interior/exterior combinations are interchanged. Beck works in business clothes at a desk on the beach. He later wears vacation clothing and reclines in a beach chair in a large office. The private functional space around the desk is preserved on the beach, a fact that we are made conscious of when a child bumps him with a small toy car. On his airplane flight, Beck, seated inside, is blown by the slipstream outside the jet, while a seagull perched on the wing seems unaffected. The idea that what we are given in perception includes functionally significant properties and relations is in line with the work in psychology of J. J. Gibson, who argued that what we are given are not objects neutrally conceived but "affordances"—humanly relevant features in virtue of which things in the environment may present themselves as potentially useful in the satisfaction of our basic needs.[6] A configuration of rocks, for example, might be given most immediately as a shelter or hiding place, a bridge, a stairway, or part of an escape route. And this perspective on perception informs a great deal of experimental work currently being done in the Gibsonian tradition.

Animateness, intentionality, and agency

In the case of the man carrying the car, the reversal of causality seems particularly salient because so many of our fundamental physical assumptions are violated. As we shall see, however, the notions of agency and intentionality are equally relevant. And, indeed, causation and hence time are implicit in such notions, as they are in the more basic notion of something being animate. The direct perception of causation, animateness, intentionality, and agency are currently under study in the experimental tradition stemming from the work of Albert Michotte.[7] Michotte studied the conditions under which one moving shape on a screen would be seen as causing the movement of another, and current research has extended Michotte's methods to the perception of simple moving shapes as animate and as goal seeking.[8] As in the case of the work done in the Gibsonian tradition, this work supports a theory of perception according to which what we are given most immediately are features of the world that are far richer than the sense-datum theory and the various camera analogies can allow.

Gondry's short films call attention to the pervasive presence of agency in our perceptual experience in a set of strikingly paradoxical reversals that constitute the subtext of many of his films. Agency, as we saw, is reversed in the Beck video in which his shadow seems to be the active agent, and he appears to be dragged along behind. It is tempting to see an allusion here to the Hans Christian Andersen story in which a man's shadow detaches itself from him and, becoming wealthy, bribes him to act as its shadow.[9] Clearly there are echoes of such important expressionist films as Arthur Robison's *Warning Shadows* and F. W. Murnau's *Nosferatu* in which shadows seem to exercise an agency independent of their owners. In Gondry's short film *La Lettre*, two images—one a shadow and one a still photographic image projected on a wall—are made to kiss, and their action seems to seal the fate of the young protagonist. And in *The Science of Sleep*, Stephane, before going to bed, lays out his clothes for the next day as though they constituted a kind of a spectral double and had a life and consciousness of their own. There seems to be a strong echo here of the surrealist classic *Un Chien Andalou* by Luis Buñuel and Salvador Dali in which clothes, similarly laid out, give rise to the double they so strongly suggest.

Dolls, simulacra, and uncanny doubles

In a variation of the theme of the uncanny double, Joel compulsively draws people, including Clementine, as skeletons and packs a life-size stuffed skeleton effigy among the things that remind him of their relationship. And whereas doubles normally appear from outside, in Joel's case the skeleton double is explicitly given as inside, though as external to the self, and hence as Other. The uncanny doubles that recur in Gondry's films and videos are closely related to three other categories of properties given in visual experience and frequently represented in Gondry's films: animateness, functionality, and the categories of self and other. This is another instance in which Gondry's other films help us to understand and appreciate *Eternal Sunshine*. In *The Science of Sleep* one sees immediately what Stephane and Stephanie have in common— one sees them, indeed, as "meant for each other." A casual reading of the script for *Eternal Sunshine*, however, would leave utterly mysterious what Joel and Clementine share or why we should see any source of hope in their reunion.

In both cases, what is shared is a strong visual and non-verbal sensibility and imagination. Joel picks the only piece of jewelry that Clementine has been given that reflects her taste. Clementine's letter in the form of a paper art construction commemorating their first night on the Charles resembles many of Stephane's and Stephanie's fantasies and constructions. A similar point applies to her potato figures. And although if we judge by the noirish and violent drawings in Joel's journal we might not expect him to respond to this side of Clementine, a closer look at the film suggests otherwise. Dolls, effigies, simulacra, and Others are not merely the subtext of the film; they are the subtext of Joel's and Clementine's relationship. Clementine learns on meeting Joel that Huckleberry Hound was his favorite doll as a child. And in the first memory Joel tries to protect from erasure, Clementine describes the ugly doll that became her alter ego and the locus of her projected self. Joel's tender words in reply are uncharacteristic of what we have seen up to that point, and the brief scene takes place under covers that suggest children playing under a blanket.

Joel's sympathetic support for Clementine as she describes her doll echoes her willingness to be depicted as a skeleton—the image Joel seems to associate with himself. And the recurring images of skeletons in Joel's drawings may not be as ominous as they seem. Images of skulls and skeletons occur in connection with both Stephane and Stephanie, as they do elsewhere in Gondry's work. And although skeletons generally retain their ominous connotations in such German expressionist films as Fritz Lang's *Metropolis*, people in skeleton suits are used to comic effect in Jean Renoir's *Rules of the Game* and in Gondry's Daft Punk video, *Around the World*. Finally, one is reminded of the comic depiction of skeletons in animation prior to the 1950s and of the role that the study and depiction of skeletons has traditionally played in the education of art students—among whom Joel, Stephane, and Stephanie would almost certainly be included.

More difficult to interpret, perhaps, is Joel's fantasy, constructed around a deeply buried memory, in which Clementine lets him pretend to strangle her. Strangulation is a recurring image in Joel's drawings, the skeleton of a hanged man being one of the more disturbing. And to get Clementine's attention, Joel mimes the victim of what appears to be a garroting in a performance that includes a liberal application of fake blood. There are, though, a number of Freudian assumptions scattered throughout Gondry's films. When Stephane is angry with Stephanie, he accuses her of not finishing her projects, a complaint that he has already made about his mother. And it is a well-known feature of Freudian theory that young children are in touch with, and manifest, not only sexual but aggressive drives. Joel's fantasy in which he pretends to strangle Clementine depicts their play and his pretence as good-natured and her response as relaxed, playful, and understanding. Again it seems that it is in their fantasies of themselves as young children capable of imaginative self-projection that Joel and Clementine have their greatest capacities for spontaneous sympathy and understanding.

That Joel's and Clementine's self-projections are often located in dolls and simulacra is made very explicit in the brief shot of Joel's puppet of a hula dancer. The puppet resembles the Balinese shadow puppets that inspired Lotte Reiniger's *Prince Achmed*, the first full-length animated film, and the image of the dancer recalls a famous image from Murnau's *Tabu*. Over the face of the doll, a photograph of Clementine has been super-imposed, and, in a conspicuous gesture, Joel peels it off as he removes all traces and reminders of her. Again one has the impression that these self-projections, like the shadow and the projected photograph of *La Lettre*, have a kind of life of their own. And it seems that Joel's and Clementine's compassionate and generous acceptance of each other's shadow selves is the basis of a deeper connection than we see in their "real" relationship and a significant part of the mysterious affinity that survives the erasure of their memories.

One is reminded here of two films in which such an empathic engagement with another's projected self allows two young people to heal each other—an important film of the 1960s, Frank Perry's *David and Lisa*, and Park Chan-Wook's recent and surprisingly gentle film *Android*. In thinking about *The Science of Sleep* in which the reversal of time figures so prominently in Stephane's fantasies, one cannot help but imagine that it represents the desire of these young people who seem, even (or especially) to themselves, to be made for each other to turn back time and begin their relationship again. Joel and Clementine, as their negative or mirror images, succeed in doing just that. Joel, as a result of working through the memories that he subsequently loses, seems to do so with a somewhat changed heart. And in light of the theme of uncaused but possibly pre-ordained harmonies in *The Science of Sleep*, we may expect that Clementine has changed in analogous ways.

Film and phenomenology

Our concern has been with what Gondry's films, particularly *Eternal Sunshine*, have to tell us about film and its relation to perception. And on the subject of film itself, I think Gondry's work is as profound as it is psychologically acute. Gondry's films reveal the multitude of ways in which the film image may relate (or fail to relate) to the space in front of the camera. And his work reminds us that the axioms of Bazin's film theory and its more recent successors define a space that has no counterpart in the lived perception of our life-worlds. The space of our life worlds is a construction—a *bricolage* or patchwork of functionally distinct zones and boundaries, making for inside/outside distinctions defined in an indefinite number of ways. Like Greenaway in *The Pillow Book*, Gondry creates picture-within-picture effects inside the frame within *The Science of Sleep*, the most notable example of which is the television image on "Stephane TV." And Gondry moves effortlessly between the animation of purely artificial constructions and the "recording" of physical reality. What we are given in visual perception are not sense-data, but objects themselves in their functional and agential significance. In *The Eternal Sunshine of the Spotless Mind*, Gondry reminds us that we are given a world saturated with meaning and with the past. And he does so through his presentation of a world that increasingly resembles the homogeneous geometrical spaces of an empty stage—a de-populated world in stark contrast to the over-populated worlds of the music videos.

In calling our attention to the richness of our perceptual experience, Gondry's work reinforces the perspective not only of a great deal of research in empirical psychology but of a long phenomenological tradition in philosophy. This is a tradition that extends from the work of the later Husserl on the notion of a life-world through Heidegger's privileging of our pragmatic access to the world over scientific knowledge to the work of such later figures as Sartre, Merleau-Ponty, and Levinas on the nature of our perceptual access to the minds of other human beings.[10]

Moreover, in their emphasis on the construction of the visual image, both in film and in the mind, Gondry's films continue the rich traditions of German expressionist and avant-garde filmmaking that was marginalized by French film theory following Bazin. Annette Michelson has written of the "options eliminated in Bazin's revisionist view of the avant-garde," options that would constitute a continuation of the "tradition represented by the past work of Eggeling, Leger, Duchamp, Man Ray, Picabia, Ruttman, Len Lye, Cocteau, and Richter," as well as the work to come of "Kenneth Anger, Harry Smith, Stan Brakhage, Robert Breer, Alain Resnais, and Jean-Luc Godard."[11] And if the work of such a theorist as Noël Burch provides a partial alternative to Bazin's perspective, the correction is far from complete. (Animation, for example, which lies at the heart of Gondry's films and is smoothly integrated with his other techniques, is scarcely addressed in contemporary film theory.) If, however, philosophy in general and phenomenology in particular have a contribution to make to film theory, it is through the critique of the concepts, particularly the concept of the image, upon which Bazin's film theory and its more recent successors depend. And this critique is implicit and increasingly well developed in Michel Gondry's philosophical film practice.

Notes

1 Bazin 1967 and 1971; Metz 1974; Burch 1973.
2 Sontag 1979; Barthes 1981.
3 Russell 1959; Ayer 1962; Swartz 1965.
4 The interview is included in "I've Been 12 Forever (Part 2 Age 12–12)" on the DVD *The Work of Director Michel Gondry*.
5 Elsewhere I have characterized such an alternative theory as involving an "inflationary/deflationary phenomenology." See White 2004a, 2004b, 2007.
6 Gibson 1986.
7 Michotte 1963.
8 Sperber, Premack, and Premack 1995.
9 "The Shadow," in Andersen 2005.
10 Husserl 1970; Heidegger 1962; Sartre 1958; Merleau-Ponty 1962; Levinas 1969.
11 Introduction to Burch 1973: vi.

References

Andersen, H. C. (2005) *The Stories of Hans Christian Andersen*, trans. Diana Crone Frank and Jeffrey Frank, Durham, NC: Duke University Press.
Ayer, A. J. (1962) *The Foundations of Empirical Knowledge*, London: Macmillan.

Barthes, R. (1981) *Camera Lucida*, New York: Farrar, Straus, and Giroux.

Bazin, A. (1967) *What is Cinema?* trans. Hugh Gray, Berkeley, CA: University of California Press.

—— (1971) *What is Cinema?* Vol. II, trans. Hugh Gray, Berkeley, CA: University of California Press.

Burch, N. (1973) *Theory of Film Practice*, New York: Praeger.

De Caro, M. and Macarthur, D. (eds.) (2004) *Naturalism in Question*, Cambridge, MA: Harvard University Press.

Gibson, J. J. (1986) *The Ecological Approach to Visual Perception*, Hillsdale, NJ: Laurence Erlbaum.

Heidegger, M. (1962) *Being and Time*, trans. John Macquarrie, New York: HarperCollins.

Husserl, E. (1970) *The Crisis of European Sciences and Transcendental Phenomenology: An Introduction to Phenomenological Philosophy*, trans. David Carr, Evanston, IL: Northwestern University Press.

Levinas, E. (1969) *Totality and Infinity*, trans. A. Lingis, Pittsburgh, PA: Duquesne University Press.

Merleau-Ponty, M. (1962) *Phenomenology of Perception*, trans. C. Smith, London: Routledge and Kegan Paul, reprinted with revised translation, 1981.

Metz, C. (1974) *Film Language: A Semiotics of Cinema*, New York: Oxford University Press.

Michotte, A. (1963) *The Perception of Causality*, New York: Basic Books.

Russell, B. (1959) *Problems of Philosophy*, New York: Oxford University Press.

Sartre, J.-P. (1958) *Being and Nothingness: An Essay on Phenomenological Ontology*, trans. Hazel Barnes, London: Methuen.

Sontag, S. (1979) *On Photography*, New York: Dell.

Sperber, D., Premack, D. and Premack, A. J. (eds) (1995) *Causal Cognition*, New York: Oxford University Press.

Swartz, R. J. (ed.) (1965) *Perceiving, Sensing, and Knowing*, New York: Doubleday.

White, S. L. (2004a) "Skepticism, Deflation, and the Rediscovery of the Self," *The Monist* 87, pp. 275–98.

—— (2004b) "Subjectivity and the Agential Perspective," in M. De Caro and D. Macarthur (eds) *Naturalism in Question*, Cambridge, MA: Harvard University Press.

—— (2007) "The Transcendental Significance of Phenomenology," *Psyche* 13, available at http://psyche.cs.monash.edu.au/symposia/siegel/White.pdf.

Chapter 7

George Toles

TRYING TO REMEMBER
CLEMENTINE

He pulled the boy closer.
Just remember that the things you put into your head are there forever,
he said. You might want to think about that.
You forget some things, don't you?
Yes. You forget what you want to remember, and you remember what
you want to forget.

Cormac McCarthy, The Road[1]

IN A 2004 INTERVIEW about his screenplay for *Eternal Sunshine of the Spotless Mind*, Charlie Kaufman discusses his intention of persuading viewers early on that Clementine Kruczynski is, all things considered, a "horrible" person, and then shifting by slow degrees their conception of her so that by the end they "think otherwise."[2] He also declares how important it is to remember that the audience rarely experiences Clementine as a person in her own right. What we see instead are Joel's projections and memory constructions of her. Since we view events for most of the film from inside Joel Barish's head, we are obliged to work with his necessarily partial and skewed version of her. "Almost everything [we] see about Clementine is Joel, really."[3] Kaufman's skepticism about Joel's and the viewer's ability to know Clementine as she "really" is conceals a strange faith that knowability is somehow more easily attainable when a different, more "objective" mode of character observation is employed. On the one hand, Kaufman would have us believe that when memory, intuition, and longing (those woefully subjective variables!) come into play in assessing another human being's attributes, the complex otherness of the person is hopelessly distorted and fictionalized. On the other hand, Kaufman implies that were he to privilege more often Clementine's autonomous point of view or simply to show situations in a manner that is not confined within Joel's consciousness (say, cinéma vérité, real time transcriptions of Joel and Clementine interacting in a balanced two-shot) we would have a much better sense of Clementine's, for lack of a smarter phrase, true nature. I am troubled by Kaufman's almost knee-jerk appeal here to the fashionable idea that our capacity to imagine those we most care about isn't worth very much. The imagination, far from being a creative means to higher insight into a fellow being's qualities, potential, and behavioral nuances, is treated as a mechanism for mainly delusive projections. Because the literal accuracy of even our most recent memories is immediately suspect, what imagination does with memory— whether through selective deletions or wholesale reinvention—is to diminish, and perhaps impoverish, memory's connections to the real.

Surely, though, *Eternal Sunshine of the Spotless Mind* is not finally about the inconsequentiality of our ways of imaginative knowing and remembering, however imperfect they may be. The increasingly involuntary surrender of Joel's creative memory of Clementine strikes us as tragic and, by the end of the film, profoundly affecting. When Joel's available stock of Clementine memories is reduced to a tiny handful, each of the remaining moments in his possession seems somehow to expand in size and telling force. Until Clementine completes her fated vanishing, Joel always appears to have a great deal of her (that is precious, valid, and *connected* to her living presence) to respond to. With the Montauk train ride and childhood episodes as my primary focus, this essay will explore the many forms in which Clementine appears to Joel, and becomes both real and unreal to him, as he, ever more arduously, tries to hold onto her in memory. I will also demonstrate how the viewer's own relation to memory is stretched and confounded by becoming a partner in Joel's tribulations. The film is continually challenging contemporary assumptions of what knowing another person feels like, and what it *consists of*. Viewers of the film are invited to reflect on the many possible ways that the seemingly formidable hiddenness and elusiveness of other minds may be successfully penetrated. The tools for this "penetration" are ordinary, easily overlooked mental resources at our disposal. For all our partiality, insecurity, fear, and inborn likelihood of misunderstanding even the most straightforward messages others send us, we have remarkable gifts for absorbing and retaining what I will unhesitatingly call real, truth-laden impressions of those that matter to us. The Clementine Joel tries to remember and hang on to in her ever-more-menacing absence has claims to reality as powerful as any other version of her, or way of apprehending her, might offer.

Joel's (and the viewer's) initial glimpse of Clementine walking on the frozen beach at Montauk in her orange hooded sweatshirt is easy to recall, but hard to get a handle on. How do we think accurately and adequately about what it is that Joel and the viewer have taken in here? For first-time viewers, the teasing half-sighting of Kate Winslet moving in the familiar light of movie coincidence to a necessary crossing of paths with her co-star is a mildly strange but plausible variation on a romantic comedy convention. Two people are out for an unlikely stroll on the same beach on a frigid Valentine's Day morning *because* they are oddballs of a kindred spirit, impelled by story fiat to collide in a peculiar setting. Although they don't know it yet, the viewer is confident on their behalf that they will turn out to be answers to each other's needs. Jim Carrey and Kate Winslet (we have not had enough movie time yet to forget their prior existence as stars) are appropriately framed together in a landscape that articulates the chill of loneliness and of wandering without purpose, as well as the quiet charm of being thoughtfully, even bravely adrift when good sense counsels staying indoors. Here are two souls who meet their privation head-on, on a beach whose stark, inhospitable beauty amplifies feelings of bereftness.

Just before Kate appears, Jim has been digging into the frozen beach sand with a stick, making a shallow winter hole, perhaps in conscious mockery of summer's carefree pleasures. In voice-over he offers the opinion that sand is overrated, nothing more than "tiny little rocks," thus adding sand to the swelling list of aggravations he has revealed to the viewer—his dented car, Valentine's Day, his job (which he has impulsively "ditched" for a spell of truancy), the weather, and his senseless decision to come to Montauk. Carrey has awakened, in the film's opening shots, to a literally blue mood—his formal pajamas and everything in his austere bedroom are strikingly tinged with it. Nothing he has yet found to do has managed to disperse the early morning funk of blueness. Kate's orange sweatshirt, which announces her presence on the beach and separates her from the logic of ice, supplies a welcome antidote to the overdetermined presence and immobilizing weight of the blues. But the stridency of orange is at the same time a slightly off-kilter approach to the anticipated relief associated with light, warmth and passion. Orange, in Eternal Sunshine, is a garish visual stand-in for heart language, a suggestion that we will have to make do until the right colors come to the rescue. Because Kate is identified powerfully with this contrarian color on her first appearance, we are given our first hint of something askew in her audacious vitality. We will soon learn that she affiliates herself with emotional values in a brashly insecure way. Even her orangeness is compromised by her aggressive "blue ruin" hair, soon to be revealed. The hair ties her to Jim's entrapment in blue, so the connection proves more worrisome than gratifying. The railway platform where Carrey briefly stood before making his untypically (so he tells us) "impulsive" breakneck run for the Montauk train, contained many inviting splashes of red (Valentine candy boxes and roses). Kate's orange is a more theatrical, self-conscious attempt to fly one's color. The happy lovers on the platform, by contrast, assert without strain their entitlement to love's largesse.

Kate's auspicious arrival on the beach, "out of nowhere" as it were, is meant to suggest, unobtrusively, that she is not purely a stranger, that in some fashion she may already be known to him. This impression of possible reunion, of a past acquaintance awaiting reclamation is reinforced as she bobs for a few moments, in and out of visibility, behind Jim's somberly blue, hunched, pretending-to-disregard-her form. He moves tentatively toward us—business briefcase absurdly in hand—almost filling the frame as he adopts the air and face of a person unmindful of an arresting stranger's nearby presence. Because he has already taken note of her and broodingly acknowledged his inability to "make eye contact with a woman I don't know," his steps away from orange Kate are those of someone not really facing forward. He is striving to stay visually in touch with what is behind him, replacing his immediate sensory field with the mental image of the girl that he is leaving behind. He has already formed a memory of this presence he has scarcely glanced at, and is keeping a tight grip on it. He is trying to stay in touch with her a little while longer in that consciousness playroom where memory and fantasy, with only the sketchiest raw material, can promiscuously intermingle.

In the next minute or so of screen time, the connection between the two stars—who are rapidly acquiring the solidity and distinctiveness of free-standing characters and thus warrant re-christening—is further advanced by Clementine's determination to be acknowledged directly. In an otherwise deserted diner, Clementine shares a secret with Joel about the illicit under-the-table spiking of her coffee with some exotic alcohol. She raises her cup in salute to him and turns him, with a single knowing look, into a fellow conspirator. At the Montauk train station platform (similarly vacant except for this pair), Clementine is again furtively observed by an out-of-frame Joel as she walks on to the far end. Aware of his timid show of interest, Clementine proceeds to amuse herself by feigning a long acquaintance with him. Held in wavering focus at her end of the platform, Clementine capers back and forth, waving toward Joel, bending backwards and making an elaborate display of her fondness, her *delight* in running into him. (Intriguingly, Clementine is granted one autonomous point-of-view shot in this station game, as she was in the previous café scene.) Joel is caught between an appreciation of the comic turn performed for his benefit and an equally strong fear. He is afraid that some matching cleverness that he won't come up with is expected of him, and that he is just a prop in her private performance. She may well be laughing at his sneaky shyness and his inadequately masked attraction to her. Her harlequin antics could even carry a thread of accusation: "I know exactly what you're up to. Your standoffish pose isn't fooling anyone. Here's something to look at, you pornographer."

For the first-time viewer, Clementine's routine at the train platform is the most persuasive display of happy-go-lucky spontaneity in her initial round of encounters with Joel. We are easily captivated by her high spirits at this unfocused viewing distance, and feel no edge in her bid for favorable attention. The look of her actions here rhymes with her bobbing in and out of view behind Joel on the beach. In both episodes, her distance and blurriness, combined with a quality of insistence in her returns to visibility, might remind us of a lost thought or forgotten impression breaking through an inner fog. Clementine's oscillating image feels like something that is not only trying to break through, but that *needs* to.

Earlier I suggested that Clementine's arrival on the Montauk beach is difficult to get a handle on. Once one has traveled through the entire *Eternal Sunshine* narrative and circles back to this misleading beginning, the sense of Clementine's first appearance no longer seems explainable by reference to romantic comedy convention. Nevertheless, her presence on the beach seems, if anything, even more ordained in plot terms when the viewer grasps what is actually going on. It is as though the Clementine memory composite lodged in Joel's head, in issuing her final directive to him before dying out in the collapsing beach house ("Meet me in Montauk"), has set off a magical echo in the *real* Clementine, which has led her to keep the assignation. What are we to make of this still elusive girl who is just *there* on the beach? We surmise that she is feeling random and in a *blind*, depressive space, as she sets things in motion once again with her habitual repertoire of ploys. Clementine is a Eurydice, returned to the daylight world with her eyes still sealed. She has been saved after a fashion by her former lover's epic struggle *not* to lose sight of her in memory (Orpheus in reverse). Of necessity, however, he has left the Clementine who stands separate from him—remote and oblivious in her own sphere of suffering—out of account. If this other Clementine has a need of her own to satisfy by going to Montauk—one that is not unduly reliant on screenwriting sleight of hand—it is a need connected to mourning. Like Joel, she is condemned to mourn a loss whose memory she has foreclosed. Perhaps in spite of all the shiftiness and made-upness Clementine discovers in herself ("I apply my personality in a paste") she is beginning to be grounded and consolidated by the work of mourning. It may be palpable grief that distills the haze around her in her first appearances, like an unshakable mood whose causes she can't penetrate. She may be more attached to Joel, paradoxically, by the heavy fact of his absence from her memory than she was in the time of loving him. When they were together, as she saw it, so much of her effort was devoted to keeping herself sufficiently well hidden that her control over love would not be jeopardized.

Perhaps mourning, early and late, is what gives cohesive form to the ego. Our scattered Humpty Dumpty shards are painfully drawn back together by the requirement that we attend (without delay) to our losses. We never seem so internally consistent as in times of maximum fragility. The bodily envelope contracts, feeling itself all of a piece as it gathers itself tightly around a gaping hole. Grief counsels oneness: it makes the unruly troops of selfhood line up and stand at attention. It has the authority to concentrate us, to reduce our craving for, our very belief in, psychic mobility. The lost attachment can put everything else we are attached to—indeed, our capacity to be attached—in peril. We have a desperate desire to make up somehow for the loss and to escape its terrible pressure. But if our having an attachment severed can bring our entire being into a state of emergency, where we have nothing but numbness and burning weakness to call our own, dare we bring anything close again? Let there be an end to abject, vulnerable embraces.

Eternal Sunshine begins by placing the viewer in a landscape chilled by bereavement. But we are led through it in such an unassuming, workaday, distracted fashion that we underestimate the severity of the psychic weather. We repeat Joel's error of treating his ailment lightly, as though it were what he calls a "funk"—a blip of "wrong side of the bed" crankiness. Joel reacts despondently to everything he encounters in Montauk, as though exasperation and indifference were the only conceivable options. When he digs his hole in the sand, he is unwittingly giving form to the hole in his memory, and his irritation at the "tiny little rocks" of sand is a stifled lament over the massive memory leakage he has undergone the night before. Clementine walking on the beach, in turn, seems to be seeking places outside her that will allow her to *picture* what's the matter with her. She tries to find image clues for what's gone missing. Hannah Arendt has written astutely in *On Revolution* about the dangers of exposing the heart's secrets to public inspection, implying that even when we tell *ourselves* too clearly what the heart's motives are we risk falsifying and even destroying them:

Whatever the passions and emotions may be, and whatever their true connections with thought and reason, they certainly are located in the human heart. And not only is the human heart a place of darkness which, with certainty, no human eye can penetrate; the qualities of the heart need darkness and protection against the light of the public to grow and remain what they are meant to be, innermost motives which are not meant for public display. However deeply heartfelt a motive may be, once it is brought out and exposed for public inspection it becomes an object of suspicion rather than insight . . . [T]he motives behind . . . deeds and words . . . are destroyed in their essence through appearance; when they appear [even if they "shine" in a "public light"] they become "mere appearances" behind which again other, ulterior motives may lurk.[4]

When Joel and Clementine first catch sight of each other at the ocean's edge—as intruding but compelling alien presences—their hearts are certainly places of darkness, whose motives their own eyes can't penetrate. The sadness of their blind mutual casting out toward false awareness (for the initiated viewer) comes in part, as I previously suggested, from our sense of a desolate grief mistaking itself for something smaller, more familiar, manageable, even dismissible. They have lost (again?) the capacity to take their own hearts seriously, and have forgotten how to discriminate between what is true and false in their own relation to feeling. While they have a chance to start afresh with one another, their complicated emotional history as a couple has seemingly had no effect (whether it is recalled or not) on their impulses about how best to proceed now. They are diminished for us if we regard them as a pair whose suffering and attempts to love have made no difference. They present themselves to an "inviting stranger" as they always did, thickly encased in self-protective deceit. The consciousness of grief, in other words, is not what points them toward each other. They do not intuit, in their silent appraisal of each other, a possible companion in grief. They have no alertness to each other's distress signals, and cannot therefore imagine this distress as a possible key to self-recognition. The "new" person is viewed instead as a relief from the burden of knowing, or being known, a light escape from the burden of heavy, nameless emotion. Joel and Clementine will turn a troubling doubt about what ails them into a trifling suspense about how to gain another's favorable attention without giving anything away.

Viewed coldly, the train scene is about two people with little available emotional capital who mimic the act of acknowledging another's presence, but with no real intention of taking anything in, that is to say, of exposing themselves to something unfamiliar. They serve up a meretricious vulnerability that, while real at some level, is not connected to any possibility of exposure *here*. They yield revelations to the extent that there are perceived opportunities for personal gain, but nothing they offer each other counts as magnanimity.

What they are least eager to let the other glimpse is their mutual despondency, as though sadness is not only a secret but something to be proudly hoarded. Perhaps involuntarily they rely throughout their train meeting on the rote expressions of their favorite social masks—boisterous and recessive. But though we can decide we *know* this on our second viewing, we can't manage to view their opening conversation strictly in terms of our disappointed knowledge. We are unable, fortunately, to get beyond appearances, and make the couple's failure to connect more genuinely interfere with our pleasure in their *seemingly* audacious "trial and error" banter. Appearances, however misleading here, strongly suggest vitality and possibility. We observe, on this screen of appearances, a gap between two strangers being narrowed; challenges being offered and nervously rebuffed; disclosures by Clementine made without obvious calculation; interest quickening on both sides in spite of missed cues, awkwardness, and Clementine's disproportionate level of aggression. Out of this extended dialogue *Eternal Sunshine* viewers are obliged to fashion their own first memories of the couple. Though we may well find it difficult to turn so much conspicuous tension and constraint into satisfying romantic symmetry, we do catch tantalizing glimpses of unvoiced needs and pent-up energies futilely craving expression. Clementine in particular seems always on the verge of releasing a true, untheatrical note that she never quite locates. She claims to be in charge of her hardedged spontaneity, but we can sense an underlying panic. We might conclude that she is bent on bringing in the burning plane she cryptically inhabits for a landing.

Before Clementine launches the conversation, Joel is shown working on a drawing of his train compartment. An image of Clementine occupies a corner of the drawing but stands out because of a light patch of orange Joel has bestowed on her. The orange spot is the only release from depressive black ink that Joel has allowed himself in any of his notebook pages that we have seen. The half-finished, still image of "agent orange" Clementine that Joel conjures up from a clandestine observation of her is arguably his least distorted impression in the opening scenes. The distant figure that he fitfully dwells on simply *demands* the addition of color, thereby rekindling Joel's capacity to feel his own attachment to color. The tint he lights upon breaks up the monochrome surface of the visual field in his drawing, and quietly asserts its power to make a difference. Clementine has not by any means re-entered his mind yet as an identifiable presence, but as a sharp outline splashed with a potent brightness she is making a claim on his imagination.

Art's impulses are all drawn, however obscurely, from the well of memory. Thus, whatever calls to Joel to pay attention and do a rendering is asserting a *prior* claim. Something rises up that requires heightened notice, and what Joel (or anyone) sees "now" is crucially a repetition or re-enactment of an image *already* seen, and lost for a time. The sun that causes an image to bloom and the "cold darkness" that makes it wilt are, as Richard Wright puts it in *Native Son*, "a private and personal sun and darkness."[5] And bound to this sun and darkness are all the experiences we have lived through and mostly forgotten, which we may imagine, in our hopeful moods, are stored (possibly intact) somewhere within us. Memory traces, however faint or invisible in the conscious mind, may yield thriving blossoms in the unconscious. And who knows what slight, chance stimulus in the daily stream of "new" sensations it might take to trigger a memory's release back to clarity? Of course, the recaptured image never returns to us in its exact original form (the original in all likelihood is an echo of something earlier on *its* first appearance). The restored image has combined with something else, in a manner that is both compelling and puzzling. The additional element is the goad to look more closely, as though seeing were most stimulating when one attempts to separate one thing from another, to lift a veil of appearances, as it were, from the equally shifty appearances beneath. Joel's drawing of Clementine is one of those rare instances in the film where an image fully cooperates with our wish that it stand still. But Joel isn't *really* giving either Clementine or her picture his undivided attention when the image *does* go still. He is no doubt absorbed in the effort to separate this image from the unrecollected thing it naggingly resembles.

Eternal Sunshine of the Spotless Mind derives much of its melancholy force from the idea of a lover's memories being wholly expunged by a foolhardy, irrevocable choice. And yet the plot also insists, with becoming romantic fervor, that even the successful obliteration of one's entire history with another person would not deprive the lost figure of a lingering, and even beseeching, shadowy presence in consciousness. Joel remains haunted (even when Clementine seems, like her namesake in the song, to "be lost and gone forever") with all the bits of her that overlap with the surviving, misleadingly "separate" areas of his life. Unconsciously on the lookout for whatever carries her imprint, Joel lives in *readiness* for Clementine. He is prepared, required to seek her anew, and it is essential, in the film's logic, that he persists until he finds her or her equivalent once again. His old ignorance and confusion are, to be sure, also fully restored when meeting her and starting over. This irony is not designed to vitiate romantic hope, however, but to give the hope enough ballast so that the viewer can partake of it. The film values Joel's final "okay"— and the largesse of Clementine's valiant, echoing "okay"—above any ironic qualifiers.

From the outset, Clementine's often abrasive, dangerous and debilitating difference from Joel is linked, in a hard to parse fashion, with Joel's *sameness*. Why must we assume that Clementine is someone whose behavior is without precedent in his experience, that she comes at him in a manner he isn't used to? Let us rather consider the possibility that she is doing what everyone who has ever "gotten through" to Joel must do, but raises this inevitable tactic to a level of irresistible intensity. She brings him "the same as what he's used to", in other words, but in staggering profusion: a mélange of demands and inviting affronts that have him familiarly, yet also novelly, at their mercy. His actions tell us:

> I need to be tripped up, confounded, wrapped in pain by someone just like you. Your face and gestures, the force that you carry, seem— as I come to know you—to be as much inside as outside me. I think you have the capacity (and maybe the will) to undo me, to take everything that I value and *hide* it in terms of you. But I am also persuaded that this imposing spirit of yours—at bottom—wishes me well, and that you're connected with whatever in my existence has seemed "for" rather than "against" me. Without your provocations and your excitement I am stalled; with them, I seem in the hair-raising process of becoming who I think I am meant to be. Even if

circumstances ordain that your hostility and distrust will win out over your warmer feelings and oblige you to leave me, or inflict other kinds of lasting damage, I cannot shake the conviction that even your committed enmity wishes me well. Your undoing of me will somehow involve whatever I have been able to recognize and feel as love.

Repeated viewings of Joel's and Clementine's ungainly conversation on the return trip from Montauk suggest how completely film narrative fulfills Nietzsche's terrifying utopian dream of "eternal recurrence." Any film, of course, that is watched numerous times shares *Eternal Sunshine*'s characteristics of seemingly fated, exact repetition. Though viewers themselves may be somewhat modified entities each time they re-enter a film's slipstream, the movie itself promises constancy, a power to retain all the moments of our previous experience in their full particularity and to unfold them in precisely the same order. What gives *Eternal Sunshine* its distinctive feel, of course, is its self-conscious dwelling on the phenomenon of again-ness, as though characters, like those in a Pirandello play, should be *aware* of the fact that they are re-enacting an already finished scenario. Their confidence that they are honestly seeking ways to make discoveries as they improvise their way forward is at odds with the viewer's understanding that they are self-protectively moving backward, backward in the order of their relationship emotions as they perform a tired dance routine that (by now) they should have outgrown. Nietzsche urges his more courageous readers to seize the possibility of living one's life in such a manner that there will be no waste or shame or intolerable tedium in the necessity of going through it all again, not just once but unlimited times. What, after all, prevents any moment from being in its articulateness, its ecstatic thereness, a "tremendous moment"—a sovereign candidate for life everlasting?

As we watch Joel and Clementine, cut off from the forgotten truth of their "tremendous moments," and bearing up under the strain of their mutual unrecognized impoverishment, we may register intermittently the hell of deceitful repetition, the ghastly trickery of time draining lived experience of meaning. This doleful leaking away eerily coexists with the security and pleasure of witnessing the pair falsely but beguilingly re-introducing themselves. There is a perverse satisfaction to be found in the bleary-eyed persistence of Joel and Clementine. It is as though Bill

Murray had turned amnesic midway through *Groundhog Day*, but had to keep re-living the day anyway. The couple forges ahead without too much outward distress through all the deadening layers of fixed attitudes and reflex response. Even the flashes of cleverness are a wearisome replay. As the two make overtures, and recoil from them, the enlightened viewer fastens on the profusion of *missed* connections. Throughout their bumpy flirtation ritual are hints of things once known and embraced that have fallen by the wayside, turning unreal because of presently unrealized, blocked points of entry to awareness and plain (indeed, simple) responsiveness.

Clementine asks, close to the beginning of this "first" talk, "Do I know you?" just to heighten a stranger's expectations and tease him with the bait of a fake shared memory. Yet her question hangs in the air with a mournful radiance and makes us especially alert to any pieces of their exchange, verbal or non-verbal, that might in some way count as knowing. How soon do we decide, rightfully, that we know something reliable or significant about a person we have just met? First impressions often lead us to write someone off *in toto* before we are conscious of knowing anything. An instinctive displeasure in a few details of another's appearance (odd fingers!) or the sound of a voice or laugh may be sufficient to blot them out. As we begin the process of committing an appealing new acquaintance to memory, is what one "knows" a partially glimpsed signal from the past? A powerful first-time sensation can, as I argued earlier, be a stand-in for an earlier memory picture. It is a summons to return effectively disguised as forward movement—an advance of some sort, but leading into the past.

Erich Heller has noted that Nietzsche's *Genealogy of Morals* speaks, before Freud, of "forgetting as an activity of the mind."[6] Without resorting to the clinically severe and overfamiliar term "repression," we might consider how the *effort* to forget (a behind-the-scenes, often virtually un-noticed exertion of will) naturally accompanies the incitement to remember. The two activities blend in one smoothly coordinated motion. An image that rises up to attain memory force takes its strength from what it drives into concealment. The activity of forgetting is the masking of resemblances. If one were immediately conscious of how the latest memorable instance is one more link in a chain of close repetitions, then it would have little chance of generating enough light and vividness to *dwell* in the mind.

The "eternal recurrence" of film experiences—a fixed order of image and sound events that we simultaneously remember and forget—shows us how, in every life situation, we play hide-and-seek in the act of calling things to mind. As a film that is familiar to us goes forward it seems increasingly clear that we know it already. Every image that appears is a further confirmation of that knowledge. We believe that we anticipate all key developments and details with unerring precision. But when we try to reconstruct a major scene accurately, say, a day or even a few hours after watching it, we are almost certain to get a host of details wrong, to lose another host altogether, and to jumble the order. Returning to the film scene to see what we have left out, we may come to the startling realization that we haven't attended to it with any care. Now that we are intent on being exact, images separate themselves from the general flow, and strike us so forcefully that it seems we are only now beginning to behold what is in them. We secure new, possibly stronger memories from a narrative that has been well digested and whose power to work surprises seems vanquished.

I am tantalized by the Nietzschean paradox of how a fated repetition of everything in a life (the old embarrassments, losses, defeats, physical maladies, and tedium that come round once more to extort the same heavy toll) might be conceived as something other than ossified, a barren re-reckoning of an ancient, closed account. The experience of watching repeatedly a familiar movie can tell us much about how experience that is always "the same" can acquire telling, invigorating new contours. Film viewing reminds us of how memory—as we process narrative repetition —keeps getting confused with other sorts of knowledge and fantasy, and of how those states, in turn, cunningly simulate the act of remembering without our sensing the substitution. We think we remember something in a movie *as it happens*, and think we recall quite specifically what happens next—and, to an extent, memory does operate in both instances. But memory also lays claim to more territory here than actually belongs to it. Our intuitive work, our casual guessing, our awareness of how genre conventions and star personae work in similar films, our current mood, our dreamy reverie of identification—all of these supplementary cognitive operations collaborate with memory as we re-visit a movie we know, and surreptitiously smooth over the cracks and gaps in what we genuinely recall. We might well be convinced that the entire experience consistently possessed the quality of a memory—of an old thing being recovered and confirmed "just the way I recollected" rather than a new thing "happened upon" and built afresh with familiar material.

In our initial viewing of a film, we are not likely to concentrate overmuch on its inalterable, "sealed in" form. For all our peripheral consciousness of artifice and of a product crafted for our use, we awaken to the events of an unknown movie as we do to the light of an unlived day. The light of our maiden voyage is akin to the light of our ongoing present tense—the immediacy of moments aimed uncertainly at an untried future. Because the future hasn't been tried and dwells, like our personal future, behind a veil, it is a *real* future as much as a make-believe one. It is a future that cannot, for all our confident guesswork, be our possession until we arrive at it, until we have had the experience of passing through it. But what becomes of this "sealed in" future once we have traversed its length once and bear memory traces of it? Can it be revived as a tenable future on our subsequent journeys through the narrative? (I must leave to one side the strong forecasts of the movie future supplied by previews.) Or does a one time future become permanently reduced to a past or a visible annex of the present? Does the very light of a movie that is repeating for us seem to be more weighed down, less transparent, acquiring something like the sepia tinge so often employed in film to mark images as belonging to the past and to memory? Second viewing light—the light, one might say, of "eternal recurrence"—is the light of enclosure. The life-motions of the characters may seem as unimpeded, as open to the winds of chance and possibility as ever, but they also bear the burden of settledness. The atmosphere in which the characters perform their actions has subtly altered. We are regularly reminded, faintly and strongly, that what is happening now has already taken place, that the characters' chances are strictly apportioned and established in advance. No further chances will come their way, though that very condition may serve to illuminate the decisions and hazards they are facing (again) differently. Things arrange themselves by a new standard of elasticity. Where do we look for freedom and the unknowable once the future has been removed from the equation, when every action is quietly haunted by the certainty of repetition, and the most pressing choices are re-enactments?

Joel's and Clementine's predicament in the train trip rubs us against the "eternal recurrence" dimension shared by every film narrative in a starkly exposed way. These ex-lovers have already done everything to each other that their narrative-ordained future together has prescribed for them, yet here they are, without foreknowledge or recollection, ready or condemned to begin anew. They do not appear to be traveling light, as so many film couples do who are poised for a giddy first collision with their fated partner. Instead they wear their joint ignorance like a massive shawl. We may regard them as culpable for their blank carelessness with the miraculous fact of the other's *restored* presence. Surely there are other, worthier openings available for a pair who, by this time, have been through so much together. They cannot break out of a winter light that seems, to a degree, self-imposed and make "better use" of this fragile and crucial beginning time.

Eternal Sunshine additionally stirs up in us—in spite of its fixed form—an irrational belief that movie time can slip its tracks and, moreover, that we, in the act of watching, can perhaps not only revise the time flow but *cure* it—as if time itself suffered from an illness. We can share Joel's immobilization as we process and re-process the film's eerie simulation of a beginning. But we feel that with the right kind of identification with him, the state of being held captive can also be a calm of fuller absorbing, so that we can rescue time (and Joel within it) from its gray, Beckett lassitude. We can (no matter how well we know the film) enter tranquilly, rather than dully, into the rhythms of an ordinary day's commencement. The ordinary day can soothingly withstand Joel's grumpiness and turmoil. With each viewing, the day we begin with wondrously enlarges, separating itself easily from Joel's increasingly small, mind-shackled protests against it. We may form a new identification with the day itself, which contains, though Joel won't see it, a clear route to his heart's desire.

Movie openings, like new day openings, can usher us into diverse modes of wakefulness. The slow emergence from sleep in the morning oddly allows us, as Joel's behavior confirms, to re-possess our own minds, but in terms that are *rightly* baffling. I want to insist on the security and reliability (underlying Joel's melancholy stupor) of the procession of drowsy, dreamy occurrences that convey us from Joel's blue bedroom to his discussion with Clementine on the "return" train. This is an ideal demonstration of how movie time can efficaciously work on us as we entrust ourselves to the waking dream of cinema. The beginning holds up impressively, on its original first viewing terms, as we learn to inter-rogate its particulars and correct our inadequate early assessments. A conflict of no small consequence arises then as we try (on each viewing) to dismantle the tranquil assurance of this gentle and right and *true* beginning (there can be no doubt after all that the movie always opens for us in the same place). We must at once *see* the beginning in its solidly specified thereness and argue against its deceptive presence, because we have no choice but to know (or remember) as well that the true beginning lies elsewhere, that what is passing before our and Joel's eyes is a false, *depleted* beginning. And yet we can also see that the day Joel is in, the day of the film's beginning, contrary to his shut-down state and gloom about prospects, is large and potentially restorative.

The present images, so composed and self-sufficient, nevertheless obscure our view of the beginning we must seek, which lies ahead of us in the narrative time of *Eternal Sunshine* but equally behind us, in Joel's and Clementine's all too well-buried past. Our task is to evaporate somehow the sense and forward-looking confidence of the beginning we visually inhabit and replace them with the dream furniture of another beginning, laden with lost emotion and a different quality of expectancy. That beginning is now ownerless, forfeited by both Joel and Clementine, and floats in the far distance—a limbo of things unreclaimable except by us, who remember what came first and Joel's pain at relinquishing it. When we witnessed the *real* start of things on the same beach (slightly chilly but not covered with snow), we could not escape the idea that every recollected—and every supplementary imagined—particular was hovering on the brink of extinction. *That* beginning was suffused, by the time we entered it, with the sense of an ending rushing to engulf it. Once vanished from Joel's consciousness it can no longer play its part as the rightful beginning. It is encased in the anguish of oblivion: a moving retrospect, fully undone (except, again, for us).

The replacement beginning at Montauk is, by comparison, emotionally thin, and cruelly dispossessed of the content that the true beginning would bequeath to it, if it knew how. At the same time, the false beginning seems pointed in the right temporal direction (forward), and seems spaciously livable—however mechanical, tentative, distracted, we judge the conduct of the couple. Knowing the film in its entirety means that we can never rest unselfconsciously in those blue and orange train seats with Joel and Clementine. We are beguiled by the circumstances and the cues to "forget" whatever does not concern the ex-lovers at this juncture, but we cannot "be there" in the usual movie way. We dizzily alternate between standing outside and being inside what we are looking at. The beginning carries unshakable intimations, for the second-time viewer, of an exhausted future and an eroded past. The present moment cries out for emotional replenishment from some other temporal quarter. Does our superior knowledge, and the secrets we possess, help us to focus this real, unreal present so that we see and feel it whole? If so, is that a way of lessening our distance from it? How is our in some ways disagreeable detachment to be distinguished from that afflicting the estranged couple?

"How amusing it is," Henry James's recurrently ill and bedridden sister Alice wrote in her diary, "to see the fixed mosaic of one's little destiny being filled out by tiny blocks of events—the enchainment of minute consequences with the illusion of choice weathering it all."[7] James opts for the word "amusing," I believe, to loosen the chains of an oppressive fatedness. She would make the act of observing itself a means of wresting freedom from the logic of confinement. Control over what she sees and how she responds to it lessens her feeling of internment in a sadly passive life. Fate opens out and becomes destiny by an "amused," fanciful re-wording of one's prospects. The "tiny blocks of events" in Joel's false beginning with Clementine have more to do with blocking and blockade than with "free" observing, or steering one's own course. It is not a matter of Joel (or Clementine) learning to see once more in potentially richer terms—the grace of the second chance—but instead a grim wiping away of the seeing process they had acquired (together) through a mixture of memory and daunting hardship. They are involved in a quiet smash-up of seeing. They move into smaller accommodations, as it were, relinquishing vital portions of the never large amount of reality available to any of us. Things flow by unstoppably and invisibly outside their train window. Inside the train there is another rapid blur of words and impulses (overlaid by the seductive lure of a new beginning).

As Joel stirs from his "hung over" lethargy, he confuses the act of guarding himself against this intemperate stranger with being amenable. He is unresponsive to aspects of Clementine he once cherished, opting instead for bargain basement alternative images of her. Mistaking these as satisfactory and sufficient, he accelerates the process of losing ground in himself. His thoroughly conventional impressions of the new, unknown Clementine confirm the dousing of the lights within him. We might well be struck as we watch Joel, like a retracted turtle, seeking to disappear into his corner of the train compartment that he is but a few feet away from the woman who has been everywhere in his thoughts for the entire preceding night. He has bestowed on her, in an increasingly expansive, open-hearted memory procession, every gradation of feeling he has ever known. Now, in hard daylight, confronted with her reality, he finds it trying and alienating to think about her at all. Something massive has departed from her in this lackluster conveyance, where he is actually looking at Clementine, or rather avoiding looking while looking, which is his preferred way of doing it. Is he less self-absorbed in this drab but *real* situation than he was last night, entangled in projections and desperately attempting to hold onto all-too-dissolvable, lighter than air, dream memories?

Proust might well have answered yes to such a query. He harshly characterized as "clumsy and erroneous" that "form of perception which places everything in the object, when really everything is in the mind."[8] Proust's narrator in *Time Regained* would likely deem Joel guilty of the age-old lover's confusion—that is, placing "in a person who is loved what exists only in the person who loves." Possibly there is some reality-enhancing good to be argued for in the wholesale removal of *all* the layers of affection, claimed knowledge and remembrance that Joel over time has woven and spread upon the unshielded figure of Clementine. Stripped of these projected embellishments in the train compartment, Clementine is at least permitted to reclaim her separateness from Joel. Why should she *not* appear to him as a disquieting stranger rather than as the source and center of his most intense preoccupations? Her present estrangement from him, and the uses he has privately and lavishly made of her, returns her, chasteningly, but also maybe beneficially, to the domain of otherness.

Do the claims of *otherness* always in our minds rest closer to truth than the claims of love and emotional need? Since love surrounds another with one's invariably distorting, if also accepting sense of "her," does one do this person a disservice by attempting to secure bonds of intimacy? Leaving another person alone, not making the effort to imagine her or "invade her privacy" by one's desire to come closer, could easily be justified on the grounds of preserving her otherness intact. While love's dubious projections have been skeptically probed on innumerable occasions, the dangers of confining people in the sovereign fortress of their "otherness" have received far less scrutiny. Conceivably the most extreme solipsists among us can be our best instructors in how to keep inviolate the otherness of those around them. They simply do not *care enough* about what others' lives might consist of to make their imaginations venture speculatively, cautiously, or even rashly in their direction. The fact is, we are bound to be "clumsy" and hesitant whenever we attempt to relate to someone in a genuine, unmanipulative way. As Emmeline Summers puts it in the Elizabeth Bowen novel, *To the North*:

> Oh surely . . . disagreements are on the surface? Perhaps between friends the surface was meant to be rough. One has to try to speak; words twist everything; what one agrees about can't be spoken. To talk is always to quarrel a little, or misunderstand. But real peace, no points of view could ever disturb . . .[9]

When decorum ceases to guide our steps, what is the value of *smoothness* in our listening and gestures? It is generally taken for granted, I think, that we can best respect otherness by being careful in its presence, and at the same time vulnerable in our awareness of "differences." But this vulnerability is also meant to be well schooled in advance about conduct that might be inappropriate, which has the effect of making vulnerability mechanical and efficient, like a smooth-running train.

Vulnerability and attraction to the other are, of course, the breeding grounds of projection, of erroneous assumptions and tender/coarse fantasies. While all of these mental activities would seem almost to insure a misconstrual (should we dare to construe at all?) of the now insufficiently *other* presence, I think that we also have to allow for the possibility of getting this elusive person right, in all sorts of meaningful, unaccountable ways. Our right readings can develop in tandem with our wrong ones, or alternate with them. Of course, however many beautifully discerning assessments we might make in the process of getting to know (and love) someone else, there is nothing to prevent the partially understood recipient of our attentions from drawing back from us at any point. Even after, say, a reasonably unturbulent thirty-year marriage, one partner can calmly declare to the other in the aftermath of a quarrel, or a change of heart: "You have never understood me at all." And how can such a diagnosis ever be disproven, if the partner holds on to the idea? At any time, anyone in a relationship can retreat with impunity to the high ground of otherness. He can insist that a friend or lover or family member who has previously been regarded with affection has no further right to claim closeness, or acceptable knowledge. Willed "otherness" can be as much an amnesic condition as love. How swiftly we can re-convince ourselves that we have always been unknowable and separate. Our sense of connectedness deserts us, and otherness once again becomes our bedrock. And we feel we are stern realists and brave truth tellers for declaring it so, and regarding everything that does not ratify otherness as dream-like ephemera. Our memories of alienation and inscrutability are clearly as subject to projection as our memories of being well cared for and understood. When we begin to distrust (or simply lose touch with) our positive memories and elect to repudiate or shrink them, what possible counter-claims could these orphaned images and sensations offer on their own behalf before fading away?

We understand, as second-time viewers, that Joel has nothing left of "his" Clementine to go by as he steals glances at a blue-haired, likely miserable, stranger on the train. To conclude that his present bereftness somehow restores her freedom and integrity as a separate person makes no human sense to me. The film convincingly demonstrates that both Clementine and Joel have betrayed not only one another but themselves by taking the "liberty" of putting an end to their relationship memories. Much of the narrative chronicles Joel's attempt to make restitution for this betrayal, to do whatever lies within his mind's power to hold onto every (any) precious remnant of Clementine. However thoughtless and pain-driven his decision to betray his memory, the cost of Joel's betrayal gradually appears, to us and to him, enormous. For us to agree that Joel's purge has some value (since it undeniably deprives him of his Clementine idealizations, fantasies, and sense of possession) is to accept Alexander Pope's ironic paean to "the spotless mind." In his poem, "Eloisa to Abelard," Eloisa briefly allows herself to envy the "blameless vestal's lot"; in that situation she could be at one with her mind, happily sequestered from the world's temptations and suffering. In her simple, obedient innocence, life itself would resemble sweet slumber, and she would carry within her none of the disfiguring marks of love's torment. But the consequence is emptiness. Preserving another from our importuning, needy selves, from our inevitable miscalculations and projections (in the effort to know her) is a specious argument for making relationships more subject to purely rational transactions—as though we would be on a better footing with others if we would only internalize views of them based on properly vetted, well-documented evidence.

There is a totalizing impulse at work in nearly all of our scholarly efforts to police and remedy human imperfection. Because history abounds in instances of the privileged oppressing those over whom they have power, not only through injurious action but through heinous ideas (often sanctioned by law), it is natural to seek solutions to the more manageable, local crimes—say, where a "typical" contemporary individual mentally abuses or confines others. The more skeptical we sound about our ability to imagine a differently situated person adequately, or to do anything on that person's behalf with the right knowledge and motives, the less likely we are to be accused of liberal piety and humanist naivety. It sometimes seems that there is no permissible way to approach others, through the circuit and subterfuge of consciousness, without doing them an injustice. We either tighten existing mind-forged manacles, or add new ones.

Nothing is more susceptible to dismantling and knowing dismissal than the piddling category of romantic relationships. Every component of them is wide open to attack, and the claims of love that are the heart of the matter grow vaporous as soon as we attempt to show what these claims rest on. Love has so much less podium confidence than power. Power is all too material in its effects and operations, whereas love is vexingly inclined to be invisible—lacking in material proofs. When a love relationship fails, what is left (or exposed) are two individuals in retreat to otherness, who have forgotten how to imagine each other generously. The gargoyle aspects of the ex-partner's attitudes and behavior are likely to be enlarged, with an accompanying freeze on delight and pleasurable surprise. The bad times and "varieties of disturbance," as Lydia Davis phrases it,[10] crowd out whatever was once undisturbing and easy to enjoy. All topics for discussion become unsafe, unrewarding. The imagination's capacity to work further transformations seems blunted. The *largesse* of the lover's imagination runs dry.

The cold facts of relationship endgame make it feel pointless to keep the many faces of the no longer beloved in play. With the contraction of the imagination's investment in "making new life" for the rejected partner, the memory suffers an equivalent contraction. Unless the lover/spouse in exile hopes for a reprieve, the memories of the relationship's beginning and middle lose the dimension of aspiration, futurity. Suddenly one knows that the terms of the relationship were rashly devised and that one entered into the whole thing blindly. What one took to be the case in the days of promise—ah, those beguiling appearances—hid from view the less conspicuous signs of already-in-progress defeat. The vulnerability that once infused memories consecrated to romantic readiness—the sense of being open and equal to whatever comes—is replaced in hindsight by a protective carapace. Memory's faith component is revised for wary future reference. A lover's trusting nakedness and salutary dependence become, in retrospect, one more liability, likely connected with the sense of having been taken in. One can (perhaps *must*) replace, after the fact, one's earlier grateful submission to another's safekeeping with a shame at having been so needy.

Eternal Sunshine of the Spotless Mind advances the powerful idea that beneath the barricades of hurt and the imagination's impulse to rewrite history after a relationship founders, there are a multitude of memories that plaintively retain the force of the original impression. Neither the static of present tense consciousness nor the ongoing urge to amend regrettable past memories so one can appear to better advantage are able to spoil the authentic memory imprints. Sometimes a writing or therapy session, in propitious circumstances, can allow us to clear away some of the dross that stands in the way of accurate memory seeing. *Eternal Sunshine*, expanding on this sort of experience, proposes that the mind may have its own way of preserving something like photographic *negatives* of events, that do not alter or disintegrate with the addition of later material—fantasies, say, or blurring supplements of changed attitude and transposed detail. What holds the memory impression together, the film movingly suggests, are the feelings (many of them born of true intuition and knowledge) that were alive at the precise instant when the memory originated. Feelings are what give form, definition, and staying power to our "held onto" images of one another. And perhaps the subsequent feelings we add to a memory—though closer to us temporally, and thus more immediate—are not strong enough to undo the feelings first attached to it. The power of the first impression or imprint comes from the fact that feeling and image were initially fused—inseparable.

An even more audacious proposition in the film is that one might be able to revisit a memory self-consciously, interrogate it or supplement it with imagined new elements, and throughout all this tinkering maintain contact with the memory's emotional truth, which is to say, the core truth. Visual and sound details may fluctuate and rearrange themselves, but the energy of their movement functions to preserve the original feeling.

If that feeling is wiped out or used up, the image field it gave rise to promptly disintegrates. In other words, the thread of the original feeling, tied mysteriously to aspects of one's life in the present, is the current that supplies light to memory details, and keeps them visible in the mind.

So much current thinking about memory overemphasizes the problem of data accuracy. If the details we recollect of any event are so often confused and unreliable, why should we *ever* trust our memories, much less anyone else's? We are intent, these days, on asserting our sophisticated disbelief in memory, because of its endlessly demonstrable fallibility. Memory's role in shaping and protecting our both resilient and fragile sense of identity is now under suspicion, as under suspicion as identity itself. I would argue that the majestic *power* of memory (as a force of good in our lives) is as neglected in contemporary discourse as the power of love. Perhaps we need to be persuaded yet again that memory and love are the most vital agents of continuity in our lives. We may not think of ourselves as committed believers in memory, but what else holds our days and relationships together, and allows us to proceed with whatever we're thinking and doing? Our commitment to love can equally go unacknowledged, and seem to have negligible weight in our conscious-ness and actions. And yet there is no shock more paralyzing than the realization that we have no source of love left to draw on: that we are wholly, desolately, on our own.

Memory makes our world visible, and the assurance or hope of love from some quarter makes it inhabitable. If there is no answering "you" for our "I," we no longer *belong* to the world. There is only an "I" struggling bootlessly to be readmitted. The sense that our existence is for us in a world that is not too remote depends upon whether others are imaginable as responsive, caring presences. As Saul Bellow characters like to argue, the "inability to explain [how memory and love sustain us] is no ground for disbelief."[11]

Judith Butler gives an arresting summary of Adriana Cavarero's radically counter-Nietzschean approach to ethics in *Giving an Account of Oneself*. Cavarero replaces the current emphasis on the constructed and constricted situation of the "other" and the "I" with vulnerability—our *necessary* exposure to a "you":

> I exist in an important sense for you, and by virtue of you. If I have lost the conditions of address, if I have no "you" to address, then I

have lost "myself". . . . [O]ne can reference an "I" only in relation to a "you": without the "you," my own story becomes impossible.[12]

Joel and Clementine, meanwhile, have not moved from their separate seats on the return train from Montauk. In an "eternal recurrence" loop, we always come back to them at approximately the same juncture, with a shifting sense of what they can do and be for one another in this false, stalled beginning. Joel is still faced with the problem of seeing Clementine impassively, without remembering her. But as enlightened viewers we are not nearly so casual as he is in our sifting of Clementine details. When we look yet again at the train episode, what Clementine specifics are most important for us to remember and how do they satisfy our desire for closeness and knowing while still allowing her to maintain a certain distance? We are still not finished deciding how we remember her—and how we can most inclusively, "rightly" remember her—in the opening Montauk scenes. Joel has tagged her as an object of interest, but one not yet clearly differentiated from the grayness of the day and the inertia in which his depression has mired him. In his lost memory life with her, she had been the "you" that gave Joel's "I" its grounding and purpose and most hazardous field of contention. In relation to her he had been frequently without border; it was unclear what belonged to him and to her, and unnecessary to sort it out. He had become more plausible as an "I" as he submitted, gratefully or testily, to the enlargement supplied by Clementine's "you." He was aware that in many ways she exceeded him, and in spite of the continued threat of being undermined or unraveling as he found himself lost in her terrain, he felt most real, most himself, in the repeated acknowledgment of "you." Her too-muchness might send him scuttling back to walled-off solitude for relief and regrouping, but these retreats generally proved short-lived. The sour perspective available in his lordly isolation was cramping and diluting for the "I." Joel, during these intervals, felt, in the words of Patricia Highsmith, "like a small silent room—maybe an empty room—within a larger room where all this din came from."[13] His returns to the daunting "you" (the dreamed "you" in concert with the real "you") "sustain [his] life in its intelligibility." Expelling from his memory everything that Clementine was for him, everything she gave to him, and perhaps most crucially everything she made of him leaves Joel not simply in a reduced state but in an unintelligible one.

On a first viewing, we might be confident that we recognize early on the type of person that we're dealing with in Joel: an intelligent, creative, socially recessive, self-conscious and lonely figure. In later viewings our dominant sense of him is as someone amorphous and exponentially enclosed. Having relinquished everything that affiliated him not only with a specific "you" but with what I would call a "you-ness" threshold in the world, Joel the subject has turned ghostly. He could be one of that multitude who, for a variety of painful reasons, never recover the conditions for true emergence with others. The key to himself has dropped through the grate, along with the whole of that consciousness he once shared with Clementine.

Joel is absolutely incapable of initiating contact with the out-of-sorts woman across from him. His shyness-declaring, nervous eye contact is more a compulsion than a reawakened hope. He is determined to be thwarted, and even in the midst of his attentiveness he is imbibing disenchantment. Clementine, for her part, feigns an agreeable mood so she can justify being even more combative when the stranger "causes" her to lose it. Clementine initiates conversation, accosting Joel in the guise of a light greeting. Her aggression during her first approach to him is only slightly veiled. "Why am I the one who is obliged to get things going?" Clementine begins to flirt—like Louis Jourdan's Stephan in *Letter from an Unknown Woman*—with a person she can't recall making love to, living with, or painfully rejecting.

Flirtation, according to Adam Phillips, by "unsettling preferences and priorities . . . can add other stories to the repertoire by making room for them." Phillips compares flirting to other kinds of "transitional" performance: "it is an attempt to re-open, to rework the plot; to find somewhere else . . . 'to go from.'"[14] What Clementine draws on to flirt with is a close-to-exhausted vein of romantic energy that, for reasons unclear to her, cannot be authentically deployed. Her overture to Joel, which is, of course, necessary for the narrative to shift direction, can misleadingly strike us as not only welcome, but rejuvenating. Clementine's flirtation satisfies the convention in which a free and spontaneous risk taker—one who lives successfully in the moment—tries to bring someone stodgy and fearful out of his shell. In Phillips' terms, her *choosing* Joel as someone worth flirting with is a commendable means of re-opening and reworking the plot (or anti-plot) of depression. Her self-appointed task is to show Joel (and herself) that there is somewhere else to "go from"—that depression is not inescapable, not an end point. His condition can most effectively be treated as an impeded longing for transition, which her energy (enough for both of them) can facilitate. Clementine's high-pressure performance for Joel is designed to convince him that her manner and slightly bizarre attire are triumphantly on the side of life. She would have him see her as the life force incarnate. In contrast, whatever reluctance he exhibits in the face of her bravado and demands for a matching giddiness are signs of a death-driven cowardice.

To focus more clearly the inadequacy of Clementine's romantic storm trooper routine, we need only imagine a male stranger taking the same sorts of confident liberty with a guarded woman. We would viscerally reject "his" attempts to crowd her without sufficient encouragement. We would be keenly aware that "he" was giving her no space or chances to react to him on her own terms—not his. Clementine's flirtation, whatever its superficially engaging "fizz," is a perfect instance of the solipsistic projection whose dangers we discussed earlier. Clementine can only see his potential use as an escape route from her present unhappy relationship with Patrick. Joel will be taken on, if her schtick is well received, as a certain familiar type of sex partner. Her friendliness isn't quite personal, in spite of her eagerness to confide. She exhibits minimal regard for his separateness, his otherness—his "you-ness," if you will.

The music that oddly breaks in at the beginning of their conversation gives us a cue that there is something amiss in the couple coming together this way. It violates a film rule that underscoring a "getting acquainted" scene is distracting, and an unwarranted reinforcement. Are the actors' personalities not strong enough by themselves? The unusual accompaniment is lightly scored (for oboe and clarinet at first, then later a wind ensemble) and establishes a buoyant rhythm that is a little tentative, with just the faintest whisper of dolorousness. The verbal conversation is prevented from achieving a comfortable rhythm of its own because the music is gently but insistently imposing a different rhythm on top of it, which Joel and Clementine can't keep pace with. Not only, then, is Joel off the beat with Clementine; the two of them are additionally out of sync with the musical instruments, which engage in happy colloquy apart from them, as if they were absent. In some sense, of course, they are absent.

The loudly striped cloth bag that Clementine digs into when the conversation yields its first overt "hurt feelings" nicely intimates that her improvisation with Joel is made up of old cast-off bits; going into the bag for a few moments may yield some other gesture or attitude she can try out. Instead of using the dare of an unplanned encounter to "rework" her story, Clementine is staying firmly within the plotline she knows best. With irritable fatigue she juggles material for interaction—rather, for self-proclamation—that can no longer advance her, that is, contribute to growth. At some level, she must know this: hence, the visible strain of her fatigue. In a speech that Clementine makes to Joel later the same day in her apartment [included in the published shooting script, but not in the film], she states that her "goal is to just let it flow through me":

> It's like, there's all these emotions and ideas and they come quick and they change and they leave and they come back in a different form and I think we're all taught to be consistent . . . It's a sign of maturity to stick with that [something you've chosen to do or someone you've chosen to be with] and see things through. And my feeling is that's how you die, because you stop listening to what is true, and what is true is constantly changing.[15]

Instead of finding ways to receive impressions in a "natural flow" or in a "different form," Clementine directs her meeting with Joel with relentless control. She is not "listening to what is true" either in her own utterances or Joel's. She is racing through her learned steps, hoping perhaps that the outcome will be self-sabotage rather than another person being vaguely seduced by her harried impersonation of openness.

The most truthful moment in the couple's entire false introduction is Clementine's elated farewell punch to Joel's arm. She may have surprised herself with the revelation that it was more gratifying to inflict physical pain on him than to convince him that her manufactured zest was real. The punch expresses her authentic underlying mood, the tension she has carried and tried to deny from the outset. By scene's end the train car has changed from one kind of empty space to a more alarming kind. The first emptiness, to the initiated viewer, ruefully attests to the missing weight of Joel's and Clementine's memories, along with all the collateral dimensions of presence and responsiveness that were sheared away with them. The second emptiness comes in the wake of the Clementine-led commotion of false intimacy. In place of a real meeting we have had an array of abrasive evasions—filling the air with shopworn trifles, refuse.

What can flirtation meaningfully recover (or rework) for a pair who have not only been lovers and adepts in each other's sorrows but who have also concluded that they have *exhausted* the possibilities?

In their new introduction they have cobbled together a drastically inferior version of their low key, pleasingly unforced first encounter. If they are to find their way back to relationship, it has to be through this desert of compromise, and "reduced for clearance" flirtation gestures. A tantalizing paradox that the film invites us to consider with respect to their degraded "starting over" is that even though strain and fraudulence pervade the conversation, their memories, over time, will find details in the fray that are deemed cherishable. If the new relationship thrives, the first meeting will naturally assume memory significance for both parties. Although certain aspects of it may come to typify for Joel Clementine's "desperation and insecurity" when trying to get strangers to like her, he might equally dwell on other qualities he glimpsed—beyond her conscious control—that prompted a more favorable view. It is tempting, but erroneous, to conclude that Joel would be misremembering his train skirmish with Clementine if he gave greater emphasis to attributes in her that had nothing to do with harshness and deception.

I would like to give their beginning time still another turn of the screw. It should be clear by now that the couple will never be allowed to escape the Montauk train. With each reconsideration of their problem of breaking the ice (in the absence of memory) something more for the *viewer* to remember and take into account crucially surfaces. Each time I try to arrive at a seemingly comprehensive understanding of how these few minutes of rigmarole finally work in the film, I realize that one more telling piece of the metaphysical puzzle has not received its due. To catch what I've missed in my increasingly skeptical evaluation of Clementine's "empty" introduction of herself, I must return to my initial separation, or half-separation, of Clementine from Kate Winslet. The promise that Clementine holds out to us for the entire length of her shabby impersonation of a free spirit has everything to do with the actress who embodies her. We must, in other words, consider the mode of her illumination, and what that contributes to Joel and our propensity to remember.

So much depends in film on our involvement with attributes of a performer that supplement the specific requirements of a character. Something needs to shine forth—or, to put it more actively, *swing out from* the actor's person—to fulfill (by filling in) the character's presence. Kate Winslet is wholly committed to rendering Clementine's behavior, physicality, intentions without special pleading or knowingness or self-protection. She would no doubt regard her performance as successful to the extent that she effaces from camera view any portion of herself that does not fuse the concerns and prickly needs of Clementine. But the camera does not see less of an actor in those instances, such as this one, where she is ideally equipped to transmit, and thus make known, a character's reality. There is always a surplus emanation from the actor taking place, the focusing of her *own* person through the "burning glass" of the characterization. Contrary to popular belief, the camera permits no real escape from certain base line truths of the performer's natural expressiveness. All good actors, but stars especially, automatically retain and project a host of flickering variables that comprise their absorbing "face value" appearance.

The major consequence of this Winslet factor in the train scene is that we—like Joel—are not restricted in what we take in of her by the troubling signs of sham and delusional aggression. We can readily sense something worthier waiting to come forth from behind the ragged curtain of Clementine's self-presentation. Emerson writes in his great essay "Self-Reliance" of the "power . . . that resides in the moment of transition from a past to a new state, in the shooting of the gulf, in the darting of an aim."[16] He contrasts this power with the condition of repose where power of the sort he celebrates in this passage "ceases." I would modify Emerson's description of transition power—which has everything to do with power in film acting—to make room for the power that gathers in repose. When Clementine makes her impetuous directional shifts, she certainly appears to be "darting" with a new aim and "shooting . . . the gulf," but so much of this energy on the loose seems misapplied, overhasty, to achieve an effect of *any* kind. It is in Clementine's rest intervals prior to her heedless lunges that she may be most attractively available to us. Her potential as a reflective being suddenly seems transparent. Her way of looking when she is not directly presenting herself to Joel suggests that she is brushing against the truth of her own unhappiness, and frankly bewildered and at odds with what she feels driven to do. She shows us, several times, that she is making her own bleak assessment of her near-hollow antics, and judging them as unworthy of her here, whether Joel responds positively or not. The best that can happen, her self-doubt may counsel, is that he will be "taken in," and that she will secretly think less of him for being duped. We sense her capacity for questioning all the things she showcases as her proud, hard-won philosophy. Repose may lead Clementine to the power of her next lively transition, but her ability to go still before making a move signals a different kind of power, a strength of inwardness—real to be sure, but insufficiently exercised.

The honesty and exactness of Winslet's performing give further evidence, to cite Emerson again, of "our vicinity to a new and excellent region of life." An actor's performing honesty blends with Clementine's flashes of introspection to suggest a giving center of consciousness that is at war with neediness and the pull of narcissism. We pass rather swiftly through Clementine's saving points of repose, but they are visible enough to insure some measure of viewer investment in the future of this couple. If we are persuaded that Clementine has something exceptional inside her waiting to be mined by the seeking part of herself (as well as by pining, beggared Joel), our memory can be drawn to the details of their "false start" in the train. How challenging it is—given the extent of our knowledge and ironic awareness—to determine what lasting impressions we form of this scene. And, once we combine these impressions, what is our overall way of remembering it and accounting for it? We should keep reminding ourselves that every occasion in Eternal Sunshine where we are led to think about memory in an unanticipated manner may warrant further attention to how our own viewer's memory, as it operates in this film, relates to our discovery.

I have tried, at no doubt vexing length, to dramatize the difficulty of remembering what is at issue and what is of value in Joel's and Clementine's false, but still real, beginning. In taking full account of our experience of the scene, we need to contend with our proclivities for tidy, clear, general statements and overstatements. We do well to balance our disappointment in the limited chances for authentic communication that the meeting offers (and our possible sense of being "betrayed" by these diminished personages) with an accompanying recognition of all the unassuming moments where illumination transpires. There are emotional excesses at work in our interpretive efforts, as well as a complacent coldness. How do we redress the force of our projections and turn the chill of a settled judgment back into dynamic, uncertain flow? The scene literally moves the characters and us along a narrative track, where eye and ear alternately catch, intuit, miss and misconstrue the objects there for understanding. The simplicity of what is going on (at the boy meets girl level) works against the complexity of all that we are eventually asked to make of it. But if we surrender too wholeheartedly to the complexity, we can crowd out the still meaningful simplicity, underestimating how much it contributes to what we know and feel. The narrative track (leading us back from Montauk) remains breezily clear and inviting until the end of the train scene, in spite of all the complications we feel obliged to build into it.

Let us enumerate just a handful of "throwaway" details that might somehow add complications to our response. What do Clementine's blue-striped hobo gloves, her blue ruin hair, or her Vicks inhaler contribute, in retrospect, to our sense of her? That is, if we decide to linger over them. Do droll or madcap particulars affect us differently if we concentrate on them separately, or if we merely register a composite eccentricity? Does the play of details knit together to form an abiding overall impression of Clementine, or does our willingness to dwell on vivid specifics usefully circumvent our arrival at a too rigid typing? If *Eternal Sunshine* instills in us a craving for a more tenacious memory, it might seem wise to emulate Joel—as he appears to us in the late stages of the film—and hold fast to every Clementine detail that we can. On the train ride, where a shared memory continent strikes us, tragically, as "gone forever," the repetition of "sacred," forgotten gestures in a tawdrier key can abruptly make us feel that nothing in the new regime of memory matters. A McDonald's is being erected on the former site of a cozy eatery where one first fell in love.

How effective movies are at shuttling us back and forth between the intense conviction that everything (every tiny shimmering particular) matters, and the drab fear that nothing does. In this they strongly resemble life. The train ride, because of its accentuated sense of "going through the motions" blindly, might seem to foster a disregard for specific actions and reactions. After all, Joel and Clementine are journeying here on a road already well traveled by them. And they do this after relinquishing the "ideal" form of the relationship lived out (and snuffed out) in Joel's beautifully insurgent consciousness. The process, in other words, that leads up to their eventual recognition that they once knew each other (and for a time loved each other) is itself inconsequential. Things only start counting again when they grasp their predicament, and either elect to go their separate ways or recommence, with the sobering knowledge of having *failed*, drastically, in their previous efforts to love each other. Their predicament also includes the hurtful assertions the two have made about each other in their taped post-mortems. These assertions have the grim finality of conclusions. How does one survive in the horrible, unforgiving light of another's "official" condemnation? Can statements of this severity, once said, be taken back or (to employ the most pointed word in *Eternal Sunshine*) forgotten?

The train ride—when contrasted with the dire epitaphs on the tapes—seems eminently forgettable. It seems to dwell outside the framework of usable character insight, and forms a transitional interlude where, ironically, *less* seems to be at stake in the living present than either Joel or Clementine imagines. Why should the train exchange matter in its own right except as a blurry means to an end—the fit end of character realization? When actions add up to "more of the same" and go by lightly, without offering special claims for prolonged attention and recollection, we might well feel entitled to let go of them, to dissolve the details, as we idly do with most of the vaporous material making up our own days and nights. Despite our many "everything matters" moods, our need to remove clutter from the house of memory every minute means, practically, that most of what happens to us is treated as though it didn't matter. No tears are shed for the bulk of what passes, instantly, into darkness. So, nothing decisively matters on the train, were it not for the fact that the scene comments so adroitly and poignantly on the distressing phenomenon of little items of personal association, bits of memory, suddenly going missing. And no one but the spectator notices, or is in a position to care. These "blinked out" associations don't objectively amount to much in the large scheme of things, but our pained response (in the film) to their not being registered bestows on them an intense *local* value.

The characters are visibly forsaking (forgoing) threads integral to their past connection, and because they are unable to hold onto the *laden* details, we must step in emotionally, as their caretaker, and do it for them. Of course, the onscreen relationship has to affect us, at some depth, to make us vigilant on its behalf, more vigilant paradoxically than we are with the plentiful scrambled and evaporated details of our own relationships. What we require to be deeply affected is a quality of presence from the actors in the train scene. I am inclined to substitute the word "might" in the phrase "power of presence." The might of presence carries the crucial suggestion of something conditional. Clementine might be present for us, say, to the requisite degree, or she might not be. And the fact of uncertainty, implying that the strength of affect must steadily be renewed or is likely to perish, is a source of the power. The might of presence, then, is either sustained by the involvement of our feelings, or it crumbles away.

Kate Winslet, a star thankfully cast in the right role, has the capacity to make Clementine ideally present to us: for Joel, and by extension for us, she is someone worth holding onto in memory. Indeed, at the risk of overstatement, she is *essential* to hold onto. Our ability to safeguard our own dwindling stock of memory treasure seems, uncannily, to be implicated in the task of remembering Clementine.

Winslet's undeclared (maybe impossible to declare) personal connection to the role allows her own presence, in conjunction with Clementine's, to be amplified, clarified somehow, and lifted higher. Her presence instructs us in how to see a person striving to emerge as her best possibility, even where nearly all the particular words and gestures she lights upon are wrong, and do not give her the desired mode of illumination. This person (I am tempted to use the word soul) exceeds what she can bring forth and manifest to others by the sum total of her expressive means. How do I conceive of you—any "you" I am fortunate enough to acknowledge—as a person? I can recognize you by your most distinctive, characteristic details of appearance, by the sound of your voice and the pace of its utterance, by your ways of being silent and of listening or not listening, by your customary and fallback moods, by your physical bearing and walk, by your opinions and enthusiasm and your manner of phrasing them, by your insecurities and what loosens you up, by your laughter, your embarrassment, your shoes, by your means of withholding and of spontaneously giving or yielding. I could vastly extend this lengthy, helter-skelter list without coming to the end of the expressive signs by which I identify and remember you. (Often, of course, one remembers something only while it is being shown. One doesn't think about it at all until one sees it again, and is reminded.) And yet the inventory of things I know about "you" does not rationally, authoritatively, organize (or limit) my sense of who you are.

With respect to Clementine, how is it that Joel manages to carry his full experience of her intact to the end of his ability to remember her at all? We do not find it improbable or disconcerting that Joel successively loses countless prized manifestations of Clementine, with all the accompanying memory detail, and yet still retains an enduring complete sense of her. As he returns to the beginning of his memory life with her, she is by no means becoming a stranger again. The might of her knowable presence survives a multitude of debilitating losses. As I noted at the outset of my discussion, the Clementine in Joel's imagination is obliged to make up for all the expunged memory detail. However much projection is involved in this work of "restoration," his imagination seems equal to the task. As Joel inhabits his final few memories of Clementine, knowing full well that when they fade out he will have lost every trace of her, he seems so effortlessly in touch with her person that we might reasonably infer that he has never known her so well. Were he to recover all his Clementine memories at this point, he would not attain an awareness of her more sure and luminous than the kind he possesses. Perhaps we are secretly relieved that a memory initially so overcrowded with images, stimuli, and contradictory impulses has been pared down to essentials. The tug of war between having and losing Clementine, of course, persists until her final disappearance, and the accelerated pace of her erasure from his consciousness proves distressing. Yet the sifting down of the relationship to an exalted, but also wondrously arbitrary, handful of "last" memory spaces (somehow encompassing everything Clementine has ever been to Joel) steadies the viewer in the midst of heartache. We concentrate with an almost god-like clarity on the shoreline limit to which Joel's memory has been driven, as he bids his death-reconciled farewell to Clementine while the waters rise and the house he had feared to break into with her crumbles about them.

Clementine is *there* in Joel's concluding memory sequence in a manner that seems integrated, whole. She seems, at the moment of "dying," immune to further distortion either by Joel's self-seeking demands or her own. She is an emanation so securely grounded (as we view her) that we are not the least disposed to quarrel with its truth. When Joel's memory was filled with fluttery, agitating Clementine impressions and experiences, she appeared to represent the force of dispersal itself. In the scatter of memory, *she* was scattered, anarchic, shifty, and random. As her power to multiply and extend herself gradually reduces, the strain of being Clementine also abates. The furious disarray of her many, hurried appearances and fade-outs gives way, for the viewer, to a more collected, abiding sense of her person. Call this person the self that coexists with the continuous tangled play of appearances, but that is necessarily obscured by them. Construed positively, as the film encourages us to do, this veiled image—which memory somehow catches and holds, under favorable conditions, in its net—is the "potential for becoming" that brings all the shivery bits of appearance into cohesive relation. It requires imagination and love to see this person and to make her (like the Velveteen Rabbit in Clementine's favorite book) warm and real. Neither direct perception nor memory in combination with it will suffice to complete the metamorphosis. "It takes a long time," the Skin Horse tells the Velveteen Rabbit:

> Generally by the time you are Real, most of your hair has been loved off, and your eyes drop out and you get loose in the joints and very shabby. But these things don't matter at all, because once you are Real you can't be ugly, except to people who don't understand.[17]

My mother, in her eighty-ninth year, is losing her memory, not to Alzheimer's but to a series of small, sometimes imperceptible strokes. Her short-term memory is severely impaired and its ever more erratic operations are a source of frustration for her, and for me as well, when I fail to remember that her worrisome gaps can't be mended by greater effort. We have always communicated easily and have been able to pursue almost any topic with humor and congenial meandering until it has been talked through. The conversational possibilities have contracted woefully over the past twelve months, and our current exchanges by phone take place on a very small, exhaustingly familiar merry-go-round. Though I know better, I frequently fancy that she is testing my patience with this new form of hide-and-seek, and if I bear with her in the right spirit she will eventually come out of hiding. Whenever I am actually in her presence, though, I feel (for a time at least) that both of us are restored to each other on our old footing.

For my part, I have the sense of being made visible by her love and magnanimity. The light of her unreserved, blissfully uncomplicated acceptance of me is as comforting a light to stand in as any I have ever known. However many tracts of my mother's memories of me have been plowed under, the version of me that her love long ago assembled has not suffered perceptible dimming. My *person*, by her light, is fully accounted for, and I feel known and understood, to the same extent as always, in terms of that person. Though nearly all our recent shared experience is promptly filched from her recollection, she is rightly confident that she is still capable of imagining me, and that her imagination, if not her memory, is reliable. What I see in her may be more divided up than her impression of me, given the different memory precincts that need to be balanced and reckoned with. Yet there is also something confirming and simple offered by the mere sight of her. None of the indispensable attributes of Rose has yet been withdrawn, or has put on an alien face. Her person, I believe without effort, is there at a glance— "in the clear," and accessible to me. Whatever it is she has always had to give so freely (in our relationship) is forthcoming from the moment of first recognition. The largesse happens in advance of anything done or said. The person coalesces in the act of being happy, once more, to see her son. After taking in her responsiveness, which makes her familiar form all of a piece, I involuntarily search her presence for shadows, evidence of struggle and dwindling alertness. Her customary strength has become an ill-fitting mask to cover her fragility, and there is more loneliness and fear exposed in her demeanor than she would formerly have allowed there.

At this stage in my reflections about my mother, I tend to recall not my own actual experiences of her loneliness but a sepia photograph of her as a six-year-old child standing next to the bean field on her parents' farm. She has often talked, in recent years, about how deeply alone she felt throughout her childhood. The full impact of her isolation seemed to her most acutely felt when she was assigned to pick beans or other vegetables for long, broiling afternoons by her overworked, relentlessly silent and preoccupied father. I remember her lonesomeness chiefly by reference to this small bean field photo, which my imagination has helpfully animated. It is not a real memory, of course, since the preserved moment occurred decades before my birth. Nevertheless, this image has a vividness and "power to penetrate" relative to the emotion that exceed all my direct encounters with her feeling cut off and forsaken.

A likely reason that this "memory" at several removes displaces other recollections of her feeling lonely is that when thinking about or looking at the photo I can stand in her place. Although I know nothing about farms and could hardly recognize an actual vegetable plot reserved for beans, and although my mother's stance and cheap apparel are decisively hers,

I nonetheless *know* that I have stood in that precise spot myself, as my mother's surrogate, and have felt identically bewildered in my estrangement from the world, and from my still new life as a child. I have also imagined that I took the photograph. I was the trustworthy stranger who gave her a brief respite from her irksome chore, and showed enough interest in her, on this lonely day, to take a picture. I can find myself without strain, or ingenious mental leaps, in both places, as spectator and camera subject. I see myself standing there, and remember what the day was like and how I felt when asked to pose. I also remember that I was reluctant to leave the child and go about my business, after photographing her, but could find no way to prolong the meeting. She was exceptionally shy.

I have introduced my mother in this analysis to give further support to my sense of how Clementine can remain a person, entirely there in Joel's consciousness (no matter how many specific instances of his time with her have been sacrificed) until his final memory candle of her gutters out. My memory of my mother being a child is linked to that extraordinary section of the film where Joel remembers an incident from his childhood, accompanied by Clementine at the same age, dressed in the cowgirl outfit she wore in a snapshot of her that has touched him. Clementine is part of a group of onlookers as Joel decides whether to hammer a dying or dead bird lying in a red wagon. The other children taunt Joel to go through with the dirty deed. Clementine sits in a lawn chair apart from the group, simply observing, but she is clearly on Joel's side. I will conclude my analysis of the mysteries of remembering in *Eternal Sunshine* with an account of this childhood interlude, and of Clementine's visit with Joel to the frozen Charles River, where she reveals the place at which any lasting relationship with her must properly begin.

With the return to childhood, death unequivocally enters the Clementine memory field. In the bird hammering scene, Joel is taking Clementine (at her urging) to the memory space of his most secret, well-buried humiliation. It is clear that this memory is so unendurable, shame-drenched, and undefended that he would go to great lengths to avoid any "reliving" it of his own volition. Clementine agrees to hide with him, for the sake of preserving herself from erasure, in the midst of childhood pain that has—or so Joel believes—nothing to do with her. They venture as a pair into a trackless region of hurt for which Joel has perhaps not found a meaning, or even a language. His knowledge of Clementine, as strong by his lights as anything real in his world, allows him to make the child that she once was an integral part of his childhood memory. She is the "you" who can rescue him from his most harrowing ordeals— by granting him the clemency that goes with her name; by answering for what he has done and making a transgression, seemingly without limits or end, human once more. She has the power to see and compre- hend Joel in situations where he is wholly lost, and unfathomable by others.

Joel's worst memories, like everyone's, are about being stuck. No sooner does he enter one of them than he is rooted to the spot of an old, but fresh affliction. Time stands still. The time that has come after the memory feels suddenly illusory, and the neglected agony resumes its grip, unabated. What does it mean, then, that Clementine acquires the power to join him in those memories (especially of childhood) where he was most hideously, unrelievedly without support? Clementine is Joel's world-animating "you," and the strongest voice within him apart from his own. His way of knowing her—whenever he believed himself loved and joined to her—is all by itself capable of rescuing him from the snares of his most galling defeats. These deep capitulations to the core weakness in one's nature are the true tyrants of memory. How simple and plausible it appears for Clementine, herself a child, to extend a hand to weeping Joel and walk him away from the red wagon, the bird he's crushed with a hammer, and the chorus of the five-year-olds' eternal, coercive derision. Joel is dressed in a Superman cape, but the wished-for invincibility and power to fly away, signaled by the costume, are absent. Any personal strength the child Joel had imagined into being has deserted him. In alternating shots, Joel, like Clementine, is presented as both a grown-up and a child, suggesting that the idea of *having* grown up (in relation to our defining memories) is itself a fantasy.

Joel's psyche is imprisoned, so much of the time that he passes as an adult, in the body of a cringing, helpless child. Little Clementine is dressed as a cowgirl because he associates that photo of her with the time that he and Clementine visited her own childhood prison and bewilderment under the covering of a blanket, with a mournful doll standing watch. While he could not perform a similar feat of rescue for her, on that occasion, his manner of listening, of creating space for her words inside him, made it possible for him to reclaim, even to love, his own fearful, "contemptible" vulnerability. He makes peace with this vulnerability by attaching Clementine's face to it. "It's okay. You were a little kid," Clementine tells him while leading him away from the wagon. She finds a small opening in an otherwise impregnable metal fence, which allows both of them an easy escape. Clementine's use of the word "okay" here anticipates its momentous import at the end of the film, where this modest surrogate for "yes" is employed by the two lovers to indicate their readiness to risk relationship one more time. The fact that "okay" allows for uncertainty as well as determination and does not overestimate their prospects for romantic victory (the second time around) makes it a braver, less vain form of assent than a triumphal "yes." In the childhood scene, Clementine's "okay" has the potency of a perfectly timed maternal intervention. It soothes the memory wound with the magical efficacy of a mother's kiss applied to a bumped forehead.

Eternal Sunshine, which spends so much time visualizing figures in flight from the menace of whisked-away memories, in this episode slows the run to a walk and shows how a stifling, stabbing recollection can be cleansed by something as basic as a few steps taken with the right internal companion. Clementine leads him out of earshot of the children's voices and out of sight of the wagon. It is as though the sleeping beauty spell of trauma can be cured by retrieving one's mobility. Time itself is re-awakened and begins to move again, away from the accursed spot where Joel seized up and where temporality froze with him.

Death images abound in the shots leading up to and away from this literally slain bird, whose destruction seems strangely overdetermined by the hammer blows visited on its limp form. Clementine and Joel take turns administering mock-death to one another with a suffocating pillow. They *begin* this game in the guise of children, in front of Joel's childhood home. For a moment Joel's young mother checks on his whereabouts and well-being from a downstairs window, seemingly unmindful that the child's game has turned dangerous. In the next moment the façade of Joel's house has become a gray, mottled, uninhabitable ruin, the doors and windows sealed against any return by the living. Joel loses Clementine and the house of his childhood almost simultaneously, while he is experimenting with a soft pillow's power to halt her breathing for good. Doubly abandoned, Joel grabs hold of his too small child's bicycle, and desperately pedals, in his frayed Superman cape, to nowhere. Or rather the riding child loops back to the scene of pillow suffocation, with a grown Clementine now astride his own older body. She presses down in earnest, his childhood savior turned playful destroyer. Joel rewards her effort to arouse him through near-asphyxiation by miming death for her. Finally, just before the commencement of the bird hammering scene, we make a brief stop at the film's most celebrated surrealistic intersection. Joel and Clementine wake up on the wintry Montauk beach in a bed that has somehow transported them there. The comfort of their blankets and their intimate proximity to each other is set against the starkly cold, beautiful, death-dealing winter landscape.

The swift accumulation of death imagery bearing down on this time pocket of *Eternal Sunshine* compels the viewer to take death in hurriedly— almost to take it in stride—from a variety of odd perspectives. It is as though we are briefly installed in a death obstetrics ward, testing death's capacity to "hatch" forms of life from its own unyielding absence and nullity. As soon as Joel finishes hammering his bird, a living bird takes visible flight from an overarching net of branches. Clementine expires within Joel, but her ghostly projections acquire more and more solidity and power to effect cures for Joel. The Clementine of his imagination works steadily to cleanse and revivify him. And her good work seems ineradicably tied to her dying out—as a light to see by. She becomes his "world entire" *only* because she is already so heavily imbued with sorrow and ash.

I have an almost daily sense of inhabiting, for a few charged moments, my dead father's body. In the celestial mechanics of memory and imagination, and the despoiling sunshine of blankness that threatens both, my father's still not completed death shadows my experience of losing Clementine. My father has been officially deceased for more than thirty years, and he now, like fading away Clementine, plays increasingly hard to get, as most of my memories of him grow threadbare and wear out. The question embarrassingly arises: why does my body so faithfully and regularly carry him in my present life, in the absence of memory detail?

Both of my "in the body" memories of my father—one connected with daybreak, the other with night—are bathroom-centered. My father would rise promptly and unvaryingly at 7:30 a.m. every morning, and his first reviving action was to cup his hands beneath the bathroom faucet until they were filled with water, and then splash his face with it. He accompanied the splashing with a ritual headshake, as though he were now firmly separated from sleep and had reclaimed consciousness on his own terms. Consciousness for him was one more routine, a well-known, easily managed set of habits. I begin my own days by imitating my father's gesture. I feel him inside me as I do it, trying his best to shake off his by now tedious death and come back to the fold of the wakeful in my company. For the brief interval that dad's effort to rouse himself overcomes me, he physically displaces me at the sink. I am beside myself, as it were, in one of the good days of my childhood, watching my father demonstrate the art of awakening.

Late at night, dad would pilot himself, half-asleep and naked, down the upstairs hall, passing my bedroom en route to the toilet. Like Noah's sons, I beheld him in his nakedness—not just one shameful encounter, as the Noah offspring were privy to, but on a great many occasions. The hallway was dark, except for the feeble glow of a single nightlight, so my father approached more as a ghostly outline than as a figure of solid flesh. But he still had the power to loom and embarrass me, no matter how many times the unwelcome nocturnal sighting was repeated. He seemed massive, soft, adrift, and mortally fragile. The paleness of his body transfixed me, and I often considered the possibility that my house was haunted by this man who—day and night—never quite knew who I was. Sometimes I recreate my father's naked hallway stagger to the bathroom in a dark house. On these occasions it is not dad's living presence that animates and displaces me, but the fact of his successfully completed death. He seems to guide my footsteps along a path he has already traversed safely, assuring me that I am indeed headed squarely in death's direction. My body is partially mine, as I stumble along, but my father, supportively, lends my steps some additional weight.

The bathroom is a friendly, familiar destination, but since it is also wrapped in darkness and uncertainty it doubles as an anteroom to that featureless site "from whose bourn no traveler returns."[18] I am learning to walk again, with my father as my typically distracted instructor. He displays a patience, however, greater than he usually manifested in life. I vaguely remember him coaching me on some lost occasion as he does now, taking the time to make sure that I'm ready. His accompanying presence conveys the message that, however well or badly I perform the death that awaits me, it will be "no big deal." I will get through it lightly. Out of my bed I venture, impelled by the necessity—dad would see the joke—of relieving myself. I will soon enough be relieved of everything that counts as me, and dad hints that he may be on hand to help me get rid of it. Just as I wake my father, ever so briefly, back to life each morning by repeating his hand motions in face washing, at night he returns the courtesy by leading me, without apprehension, a bit closer to death's door.

I am thus gathering new memories of my father as tutor and guide, in much the same fashion that Joel does with Clementine. She helps him, once he gets past the barrier reef of their recent acrimony, in all the ways he imagined, early in their relationship, she would be capable of helping him. He was no doubt correct in these intuitions of her potential. Whose fault is it really that she did not more often find chances to be the attentive, emotional provider? Perhaps Joel forgetting his own prior belief in her power to be *many* versions of herself in her relation to him is partly what disabled and marked her. Remembering that she could be *more* than her disgruntlement, her defensive hostility, and her "train wreck" narcissism (as he does in his struggle against the erasure process) is a means of bringing her back into the open. A bad set of appearances can so easily block our view and memory of a better set. One needs to stay imaginatively in touch with the always renewable conditions of the "better set," and by keeping faith with their reality, believing them into being. As Joel's memory of Clementine learns to breathe freely again (strangely, in the very midst of crisis), her propensity for kindness and generosity breathes along with it. The radiance in her that he had somehow lost the knack of drawing forth in the stalemate phase of their time together emerges once more as a salient and effortless attribute. It blends in with everything else about her that he remembers/imagines/ knows to be the case.

The first time in the film where we see Joel and Clementine get past the strain of not quite fitting together, of not having a good couple's harmonious rhythm, is when they lie on the frozen Charles River, beside a starburst of subdued yet still treacherous crack lines in the ice surface. It is our initial glimpse of them relaxing together (after the false beginning on the train). They are relaxed enough to be still and alert to each other's signals, without forcing it. The two are not looking at each other. They are gazing upward at the chill, sparkling heavens, which *we* do not see directly, but which are brought to us by proxy through the ground level flow of winking car lights on the far shore. The Charles River memory is about being together without the need to watch each other, and seeing something together that is taken hold of by free, playful imagining. Joel makes up a constellation named Osidius, and makes it real by his emphatic description of the "swoop and cross" of the aligned stars. Once Clementine agrees to see it his way, the constellation is there for them both to identify and remember. We feel closer to the pair emotionally in this scene than at any previous point in the narrative, but paradoxically the camera keeps them at a distance. We survey their intimacy from the height of a lengthy overhead long shot.

Joel has overcome his initial deep reluctance to be on the ice. He is no longer worrying about how far out he is or of his need to get back or of the isolation of the spot. The ice could conceivably give way at any moment (what a thin surface divides him from death), but Joel's accept-ance of the fact that it is holding his weight for now and that that is all of the safety possible or required, centers him. Acceptance makes him a vessel for Clementine's presence and brings all the mismatched parts of him momentarily together. He forms an image of Clementine in his head that he can see without having to look at her. As this imaginative memory is planted, he also gains the power to see himself in love with her. Although he has just fallen in love with her, he can already regard the doing of it as a memory of long standing. Clementine likes to take all of her boyfriends out to the frozen Charles River so she can give them (she thinks) a special sense of the danger a relationship with her will surely entail, but also of the conceivably large rewards a lover will get for persisting. For her to find a contented stillness, there must first be an ice pillow and a bed of drowning beneath her. The experience of *everything* suddenly giving way, being taken away, is what the Velveteen Rabbit needed to become real. Clementine finds it more difficult to become real to herself than to convince *others* that she is real. The Charles River is both a fantasy location for her and a place so allied to extremity that it somehow forces reality—that is, a sense of her own reality—to break through.

It is important for *Eternal Sunshine*'s memory scheme that the river episode doesn't belong exclusively to Joel and Clementine. Clementine has made so many visits to this place, and in such diverse company, that it may well border (for her) on the commonplace. Even the authentic dangers have become, occasionally, pedestrian and routine by dint of repetition. So the uniqueness of the circumstances in which Joel and Clementine discover they may be right for each other is interestingly called into question without jeopardizing the truth of the feelings that are released there. The magic is enhanced rather than undone by the suggestion that Clementine's gift to Joel is a trifle worn and stale. It is another case of lovers making fresh, tingling memories out of their rapt beholding of a moon shining just for them. The film lets us know, repeatedly, that there is always something frayed and blank in the materials making up even the most hallowed memories, which the imagination must fill out.

My mother's picture of me as her memory continues to fail may itself turn (may already have turned) raggedy, pale, and formulaic. The crowd of my defining particulars disassembles as my mother's attachment shifts over more and more completely to an enduring idea, or sense, of my person (the son who has for so long been an essential "you"). The idea of me is wispily ratified by whatever details I may pleasingly project at any given moment on the phone or in her presence. She often wants to end conversations quickly for fear of not engaging my interest honestly. I am a set of loose reminders, most of them agreeable but swiftly released from memory like a flock of sparrows, almost at the moment of contact. I return to the photo of my mother as a child in the bean field, where, as I have already mentioned, I continually find myself present: as a companion for the lonely girl (close and unnoticed as her crimped shadow), and as a figure hidden behind her eyes, peering out with her at the desolate, friendless, oppressively hot morning. The bean field could be regarded as a version of the Charles River memory. The distance of the camera from the still, recumbent pair in *Eternal Sunshine* seems to turn space into time, an effect shared by my view of my unexpectant, resigned mother, disguised as a child.

If I am not visible in the photo beside my mother, or superimposed upon her, it may be because I have just faded out, as Clementine so often does after one of Joel's memories of her disintegrates. But I struggle to project myself there just the same, as I have done so often before, to hold onto my flimsy place. I want to assuage her loneliness, by coming toward her like a cheerful emissary from her future, where the best part of our time together was situated, before so much that counted for something was used up. "Rose, you will soon open your life to fun and friendship, and there will come a time when the bean field is lost sight of, as the intractable reality of your situation. The scene will be alive with warm, importunate faces before the friends have mostly died and you take up the familiar pose again at an advanced age, gazing outward, chewing your lower lip, as I find myself doing while absorbing your 'unfinished' image and trying to remember something or someone that could reduce your privation." She acknowledges the camera, she knows what she has to do until the shutter clicks—she must try to look pleasant, and call to mind a comforting thought that has nothing to do with the morning chores ahead of her. She tries to make a space in advance, for memory to fill, to put a version of herself in play that when encountered later on will relate to openness and possibility, to finding the loving "you" who could banish the day's sadness. She daydreams of looking back on this happiness-enhanced image together with this barely imaginable "you," and having the power then to break the lonely spell. The bean field sunshine will be beneficent, even eternal, if that wish could be granted.

Notes

1 McCarthy 2006, p. 12.
2 Kaufman 2004, p. 141.
3 Kaufman 2004, p. 135.
4 Arendt 1990, p. 96.
5 Wright 2005, p. 29.
6 Heller 1988, p. 177.
7 James 1989, p. 41.
8 Proust 1983, pp. 950, 972. Rae Langton's unpublished essay, "Projected Love," drew my attention to this quotation.
9 Bowen 1979, pp. 203–4.
10 Davis 2007.
11 Bellow 1970, p. 236.
12 Butler 2005, pp. 32–3.
13 Highsmith 1988, p. 37.
14 Phillips 1994, p. xxv.
15 Kaufman 2004, pp. 19–20.
16 Emerson 1983, p. 271.
17 Kaufman 2004, p. 57. The Velveteen Rabbit references appear only in the published screenplay. They have been cut from the completed film.
18 Hamlet, Act III scene 1.

References

Arendt, Hannah (1990) On Revolution, New York: Penguin Books.'
Bellow, Saul (1970) Mr Sammler's Planet, New York: Viking.
Bowen, Elizabeth (1979) To the North. New York: Avon.
Butler, Judith (2005) Giving an Account of Oneself, New York: Fordham University Press.

Davis, Lydia (2007) *Varieties of Disturbance*, New York: Farrar, Straus and Giroux.

Emerson, Ralph Waldo (1983) *Essays and Lectures*, New York: The Library of America.

Heller, Erich (1988) *The Importance of Nietzsche: Ten Essays*, Chicago, IL: University of Chicago Press.

Highsmith, Patricia (1988) *The Tremor of Forgery*, New York: The Atlantic Monthly Press.

James, Alice (1989), quoted in Christopher Bollas, *Forces of Destiny: Psychoanalysis and Human Idiom*, London: Free Association Books.

Kaufman, Charlie (2004) *Eternal Sunshine of the Spotless Mind: The Shooting Script*. New York: Newmarket Press.

McCarthy, Cormac (2006) *The Road*, New York: Vintage.

Phillips, Adam (1994) *On Flirtation: Psychoanalytic Essays on the Uncommitted Life*, Cambridge, MA: Harvard University Press.

Proust, Marcel (1983) *Remembrance of Things Past*, Vol. 3 [*The Captive; The Fugitive; Time Regained*], trans. C. Scott Moncrieff and Terence Kilmartin, and by Andreas Mayor, New York: Penguin.

Wright, Richard (2005) *Native Son*, New York: Harper Perennial.

Index